2025
ERIC HOFFER AWARD
Business Category Finalist

Praise for:

The Visionary Leader: The Success Principles of The World's Greatest Visionaries

"*The Visionary Leader: The Success Principles of The World's Greatest Visionaries* goes beyond most discussions of leadership to inject the concept of vision into the process. While this addition may initially seem like a small adjustment, in fact, it represents a big divergence from many books about leadership, in that it promotes visionary thinking as a major part of the leadership process.

Historical figures, practical applications, and how new Visionary Leaders should employ mentoring, seek collaborative opportunities, and absorb community evolutionary processes translates to not just influencing, but sparking enthusiasm among team members. The result is a hard-hitting, uncommon survey as vivid as it is enlightening

Bryan Smeltzer's advice can be applied to a range of situations beyond the usual business focus of leadership, whether organizational in nature or introspective analyses of personal goals and dreams. Smeltzer clearly outlines the features that differentiate the visionary leader from one who adopts basic techniques for guiding others."

Diane Donovan, Senior Reviewer,
Midwest Book Review

"*The Visionary Leader* offers actionable advice to apply to your life and career, whether you aspire to define your vision, lead organizations, or pursue your lifelong dream.

By showcasing these real-life examples of Visionary leaders who have overcome adversity and achieved remarkable success, the book empowers readers to embrace their potential and pursue their dreams with courage, resilience, and purpose.

By illuminating the transformative power of Visionary leadership, you can walk away inspired, informed, and empowered to become a catalyst for positive change in your life and your world."

Sr. Critic Review,
The BookLife Prize
(Publishers Weekly)

"The time-tested advice, combined with an approachable and engaging narrative style, makes this book critical for success.

Since the book's legendary figures span centuries, their accomplishments and approaches are evaluated against the climate of their era, providing a time-adjusted lens through which their influence can inspire innovative solutions to the complex challenges we face today. This interesting exploration fleshes out many iconic leadership legacies while highlighting imitable qualities that can be found across these visionaries.

What can readers expect to take away from this lively guide? An exemplary framework emerges, one that makes intentional leadership an opportunity to inspire and achieve meaningfully envisioned change.

The ability to learn from failure, the drive to innovate and pivot as needed, and the value of bold risk-taking are among the core ideas examined in this motivational book."

Nicky Flowers,
Indies Today

"Drawing on historical and modern leaders like Steve Jobs, Albert Einstein, and Marie Curie, Bryan Smeltzer's *The Visionary Leader* presents a perceptive study of the ideas that define visionary leadership. Through extensive case studies and practical applications, the book underlines the need of creativity, resilience, and strategic foresight in leadership. It acts as both a manual and an inspiration for future visionaries to develop a transforming attitude and have a long-lasting impact."

Indie Reader

"An insightful exploration of the minds and methodologies of some of history's most influential figures. Smeltzer meticulously details the traits and practices that characterize visionary leadership, creating a manual for anyone aspiring to lead with impact and innovation."

Carol Thompson,
Readers Favorite

"*The Visionary Leader* addresses your mindset and how you can develop ideas by altering your thought process to produce original, fresh designs and concepts. Through sixteen DNA visionary aspects, Bryan Smeltzer shows how purpose-driven leaders have created and maintained companies."

Courtnee Turner Hoyle,
Award Winning Author

"*The Visionary Leader* content is rich in wisdom, Smeltzer's focus on individual growth and innovation pushes his work beyond the theoretical and makes this book a call to action for anyone looking to lead with purpose and impact. Very highly recommended."

Asher Syed, Sr. Reviewer

"Drawing lessons from Steve Jobs, Leonardo da Vinci, Albert Einstein, Nikola Tesla, Marie Curie, Martin Luther King Jr., and more, this book serves as an essential playbook for aspiring leaders, entrepreneurs, and innovators.

Smeltzer brilliantly dissects the DNA of visionary leadership, covering 16 core principles that define success—from vision and passion to risk-taking, adaptability, and resilience."

Sr. Reviewer,
BookSprout

THE VISIONARY LEADER

The Success Principles of the World's Greatest Visionaries

Bryan Smeltzer

LIQUIDMIND PRESS

Smeltzer, Bryan, The Visionary leader: The success principles of the
world's greatest visionaries / Bryan Smeltzer.

ISBN: 978-1-7371881-2-4

Published in the United States of America

First published in 2024 by LiquidMind Press

This book is for leaders who aspire to be Visionaries.
Let your past enlighten you, envision your future, and
become what you dream of.

Set your vision.
Plan your journey.
Walk your path.
Realize your dream.

CONTENTS

INTRODUCTION

In the 1990s, despite previous success in building the personal computer market, the Apple Corporation was on the edge of bankruptcy, ready to fall off a cliff. The company struggled with declining sales, financial deterioration, market share losses to inferior competitors, and a lack of innovation in its product pipeline.

How did things get so bad, and how could Apple possibly return from the edge of the cliff? To find that answer, we must do what Apple did at that critical, life-or-death moment: look backward to find a way forward.

In the 1980s, Steve Jobs co-founded Apple with Steve Wozniak and Ronald Wayne. After founding the company and leading it from a start-up to global leadership in the computer industry, internal conflicts and disagreements with executives and the board led Jobs to depart in 1985. Soon after leaving Apple, Jobs founded NeXT Computer and acquired The Graphics Group, which later became Pixar Animation Studios. Although NeXT did not achieve meaningful industry success, Pixar became a significant player in the animation industry, and the NeXT operating system was best in class.

On the verge of collapse in 1997, Apple acquired Jobs' NeXT for its NeXTSTEP operating system and, as part of the deal, brought Steve Jobs back into the company's core leadership. Jobs returned initially as an advisor, but it became clear that the company needed a foundational leadership change.

As interim CEO, Jobs quickly initiated a series of changes to revitalize and inject the old Apple culture into the company. He streamlined Apple's product line, building a two-tier product layer—one for business and one for the consumer. He focused on category innovation and disruption and, perhaps most importantly, introduced the "Think Different" marketing campaign.

What was so special about this new slogan? With these two simple words, Jobs ingrained the idea in Apple's workforce and its consumers alike that they are "different." This simple idea changed how people thought about computers and how they use them. Apple committed itself to "thinking different," not only by imagining and realizing a different future than the bleak one ahead of them, but by conceptualizing their labors as part of an ongoing story of disruption and innovation. Under Jobs' direction, Apple as an organization collectively began to honor those who had come before, faced similar challenges, and overcame them. Jobs' words are iconic, and the message is simple to understand:

> "Here's to the crazy ones. The misfits. The rebels. The troublemakers. The round pegs in the square holes. The ones who see things differently..."
>
> **– Steve Jobs**

One of the critical moments during this time was the introduction of the iMac in 1998. This colorful and innovative desktop computer immediately drew everyone into Apple's new core product line and disruptive mindset. The global success of the iMac marked the beginning of Apple's resurgence back to the top of the computer industry.

Under Jobs' leadership, Apple continued to innovate, introducing iconic products like the iPod, iPhone, and iPad. These products revolutionized the cell phone, portable computing, and music industries, and solidified Apple's position as the most disruptive brand on the planet. Continuous product innovations, progressive updates, and culture building at its core made Apple what it is today: the most valuable brand in the world!

Steve Jobs' return to Apple is credited with saving it from potential bankruptcy and transforming it into the world's most valuable and influential company. Jobs' vision, leadership, and commitment to innovation played a crucial role in shaping Apple's success into the 21st century, and his actions at this time set the standard for how a Visionary leader behaves.

What Is Visionary Leadership?

Visionary leadership is a leadership style in which a leader has a clear vision of the future, communicates that vision to others, and inspires and motivates people to work toward achieving that vision. Visionary leaders are forward-thinking, innovative, and able to see the bigger picture. They deeply understand their brand, industry, and community, and can anticipate both future trends and the challenges standing in the way of executing their vision.

Visionary leaders can come from any walk of life and any culture in the world, and history has produced a vastly diverse range of Visionary leaders in fields ranging from entrepreneurship and business to art, politics, philosophy, defense, and more. In researching some of the most famous and the little-known Visionary leaders of all time, I found a great deal of difference in how these individuals lived their lives and applied their remarkable talents. I also found that Visionary leaders possess a unique set of 16 qualities and principles that enable them to inspire and guide others toward a shared vision of the future, collectively making up the DNA of Visionary leadership.

What Is in the DNA of the Visionary Leader?

- **Vision** | Visionary leaders have a well-defined and compelling vision of the future. They have a clear direction of where their brand or organization is going and the ability to articulate this future.
- **Mindset** | Visionary leaders control their minds to devise and execute ideas that address real-world issues. They explore the current day status quo and futurecast Visionary outcomes, executing a relentless strategy to move beyond the static circumstances.
- **Ideas** | Visionary leaders have an internal desire to change the world for the better, to make things easier with simple sophistication. They are always building a pipeline of new ideas and innovations, encouraging creativity and experimentation within their organization, and creating a culture of innovation.

- **Passion** | Visionary leaders inspire and motivate their followers. They are passionate about their vision, sharing this future and empowering others to realize it.
- **Insight** | Visionary leaders think strategically and show incredible insight into complex scenarios. They identify opportunities and anticipate threats, formulate clear strategies, and plan for the long term. They proactively anticipate changes in the external environment and adapt their vision and strategies accordingly.
- **Reality Distortion** | Visionary leaders build a brand culture of relentless innovation and creativity within their brand, creating the new reality to which their vision belongs. They embrace risk, reward failures, and encourage new ideas or a different way of thinking and doing.
- **Commitment** | Visionary leaders commit their efforts to continual, incremental improvement of themselves as leaders and as individuals. They carry out daily affirmations in which they rededicate themselves to their vision and values, which are their foundation.
- **Relentlessness** | Visionary leaders are relentless in the face of setbacks. They can quickly pivot their plans and strategies in response to changing circumstances without losing sight of their vision, and they refuse to give up on what's important to them.
- **Machine-Like Precision** | Visionary leaders define and implement successful strategies with ease, inspiring their teams to take necessary actions for brand success. They remain flexible in the face of changing circumstances and mobilize their teams to overcome any challenges.
- **Risk-Taking** | Visionary leaders are fearless in taking risks and finding unconventional solutions to everyday problems.

They are willing to take risks and step outside their comfort zones, and they have the courage to pursue unconventional ideas, even in the face of uncertainty and criticism.

- **Ability to Learn from Failure** | Visionary leaders are resilient in facing challenges and setbacks. They remain determined and focused on their vision, even during difficult times. They view failures as learning opportunities and use them to grow and improve.

- **Carrying the Torch** | Visionary leaders maintain their link to leaders who have paved the way before them, both in their organization or field and for the world. They proudly carry the torch for visionaries who have gone before and maintain a legacy they can pass on to the next generation.

- **Embodying the Soul of their Organization** | Visionary leaders lead with integrity and foundational ethical standards. They are honest, transparent, and fair in their dealings with others. Their actions align with their words, earning them the trust and respect of their followers.

- **Isolation** | Visionary leaders are aware of their own isolation as unique individuals and can navigate their loneliness and the emotions of those around them. They understand their own needs and the needs of team members and stakeholders, building strong relationships based on trust and mutual respect.

- **Faith** | Visionary leaders are characterized by their ability to define a vision for the future, set ambitious goals, and motivate others to achieve it. They demonstrate high confidence in their ideas, even when uncertain or challenging. Most will have a belief anchored in faith in God and the possibility of a better future.

- **Dedication** | Visionary leaders dedicate their lives to the well-being of the world. They are tireless and selfless in pursuing goals that will improve society at large, taking inspiration from great Visionary leaders before them.

By embodying these principles, Visionary leaders can inspire and lead their teams toward a future that aligns with their shared generational vision. In my previous book *The Visionary Brand*, I laid out exactly what sets iconic, world-changing companies like Apple and Adidas apart from ordinary organizations. Now, in *The Visionary Leader*, we will study the traits of Visionary leaders, their core characteristics, and the principles that have allowed them to succeed in business and life. Each aspect of Visionary DNA will be explored in detail, then examined in a case study of one or more leaders who exemplified this trait in their life.

Over many years, I have been fortunate to have worked with, met, or ingrained myself in what makes these leaders tick and how they consistently generate and execute a vision so few can achieve. Now, I choose to share what I've learned with you so you, too, can bring your own vision to life for the betterment of the world.

Welcome to the ranks of Visionary leadership.

Chapter 1 | The VISION

"A vision without action is a daydream. Action without vision is a nightmare."
– Soichiro Honda, Founder of Honda Motors

All Visionary leaders have the inherent ability to set a vision of the path forward envisioning where the brand will be in five or ten years, imagining a course no one can see, and being able to translate how it will be achieved. They must then communicate to all who are part of the brand team a passionate vision and an inspiring picture of a future that aligns with the brand's foundational principles.

They are opposed by the naysayers—the unbelievers, those who must "see it to believe it"—and are bolstered by believers, those brand torchbearers who "believe it before they can see it." While caution is an important virtue in its own right, Visionaries are recognized and celebrated for their boldness, not their hesitation; believers know what it takes to succeed, and naysayers play it safe. Nothing significant would have ever been accomplished without the Visionaries and those who believe in them.

Vision Is Adaptable

Visionary leaders focus on developing a long-term vision for their brand or company—but any long-term plan must be responsive to changes that may arise further down the road. However revolutionary their ideas might be, a leader's vision is only as good as their ability to anticipate what lies ahead and avoid the landmines along the way. They continually analyze external factors such as technological advancements, market trends, social changes, and geopolitical shifts. This helps them identify potential opportunities and threats.

This key Visionary element is the practice known as *futurecasting*. Broadly defined, futurecasting involves anticipating potential challenges to achieving a goal and accounting for them before they can happen—in other words, it's the necessary ingredient that turns a daydream into a vision. Few possess such a skill, and most Visionaries lead their brands to successfully execute a step-by-step futurecasting strategy for building long-term generational growth.

Visionary leaders use futurecasting as a strategic approach to shape both their brand's future and a plan for its successful execution. Futurecasting involves envisioning potential disruptive or innovative scenarios identifying trends and product or service developments to determine the path forward. These trailblazers futurecast in order to set the course for others to follow, continually finding ways to think outside the status quo and move their industry forward.

Sun Tzu, the brilliant Chinese military strategist and philosopher, wrote in his celebrated book *The Art of War* how a leader's vision can be used to their side's advantage.

The supreme art of war is to subdue the enemy without fighting.
To know your Enemy, you must become your Enemy.
In the midst of chaos, there is also opportunity.
The greatest victory is that which requires no battle.

The art of war teaches us to rely not on the likelihood of the enemy's not coming, but on our own readiness to receive him; not on the chance of his not attacking, but rather on the fact that we have made our position unassailable.
- Sun Tzu

These quotes reflect Sun Tzu's strategic and philosophical insights on warfare, leadership, and the importance of understanding oneself and your adversary (in a business setting, your competition).

Futurecasting is one of a Visionary leader's most valuable assets in their arsenal. They deploy it when they envision their brand's future, anticipate potential moves, and make it part of their strategic planning process. Being prepared for battle is as crucial as the battle itself. By considering these various possibilities, they can develop adaptable and resilient strategies in the face of uncertainty.

Vision Is Innovative

Vision drives how a leader determines what is needed before it is wanted. Sure, your consumer will always *want* the next generation, but *need* is driven by the vision of the future. Disruption and innovation are vital ingredients to executing a leader's vision.

Leaders are willing to take significant risks and encourage a culture of valuing experimentation. This allows the organization to test new ideas and learn from successes and failures.

These Visionaries set their vision with strategic foresight, which involves systematically anticipating the future and potential disruptions. This approach helps them to make decisions based on a deep understanding of the evolving global landscape.

At the same time, emphasizing innovation is crucial to setting a leader's vision. Visionary leaders encourage a culture of innovation, fostering creativity, adapting what has worked in other market segments, and making it your own. This enables your brand to maintain and sustain your category leadership position continually.

In maintaining a brand leadership position, being ahead of the technology curve is always a challenge. Visionary leaders embrace emerging technologies and understand their potential impact on the industry and the brand. They invest in research and development to stay at the forefront of technological advancements and ensure that whatever the investment, the brand will be more successful and its teams will be more efficient.

Vision Is Focused

Visionary leaders set their vision of the future through a combination of strategic thinking, continual idea generation, and an understanding of the current landscape of the brand. These are the foundational building blocks for anchoring a brand to achieve its goals. Unlike the majority that chase current trends, Visionaries focus on these foundational building blocks and stick to the most critical tasks. This focus keeps them on a path to execute their vision—always one step at a time, moving forward even in the face of eventual setbacks. Storms come and go, but your focus should always stay on your destination.

Visionaries understand the state of their business across all tangible and intangible levels. The tangible is revenue, profits, team members, community, and external environment. The intangibles are your culture, mindset, and internal environment. Determining the health and heartbeat of the brand is an intuitive skill of Visionaries, a component of their focus of vision. They can gauge the company's pulse through the reality of their lenses, a reality check, or through others who provide answers to specific questions. The Visionary puts the puzzle pieces in place and provides insight into the future vision through present-day reality. They anticipate new trends, proactively identify opportunities, and anticipate challenges, always optimistically expecting the best and being prepared for the worst.

Visionary leaders approach thinking about their company's future success with a strategic and forward-looking mindset. We will discuss this mindset throughout *The Visionary Leader* in order to provide insight into the perspective of a Visionary leader and how they create and execute the future vision of their company. In addition to the above traits (adaptability, innovation, and focus), there are many key areas of leadership inherent in vision, some obvious, some less so; however, each is a priority in how Visionary leaders construct and manifest their vision:

Planning | Visionary leaders have a clear, concise focus on strategic planning, considering the company's long-term goals and objectives. They are to communicate a roadmap for success, outlining the steps and initiatives needed to achieve their vision.

Culture | Visionaries foster a culture of creativity and inclusiveness, embrace risk, encourage new ideas, and reward progressive failures. They drive an intentional desire to crush the competition and build a cultural DNA embraced by the company for the betterment of the brand. Visionary leaders envision a brand in which employees are continually engaged, challenged, rewarded, motivated, and aligned with the company's values, each contributing to its long-term success.

Trends | Visionary leaders continuously monitor market trends and industry disruptions. They proactively identify shifts in community actions, category innovations, and other industry forces that could impact the brand.

Community Focus | Visionary leaders recognize the importance of exceeding customer expectations. They anticipate what their customers need and innovate in creating products and services that satisfy current demands and foresee future preferences.

Team Investment | Visionary leaders know future success is tied to the talent within the brand. That's why they invest in building brand culture, recruiting, developing, and retaining skilled team members who can influence the brand's growth curve, create disruptive innovation, and build future generations of leaders.

Global Perspective | Visionary leaders monitor the global environment. They interpret how worldwide geopolitical, economic, and social factors might affect their company and its success.

Risk Assessment | Visionary leaders take risks and emphasize risk assessment in their organizations. They assess potential challenges and develop strategies to reduce risks that could threaten the company's long-term success. While risk assessment is needed, taking the risk is imperative.

Technology | Visionary leaders understand the role of technology in shaping the brand's future. They determine what is required long before it is needed and integrate innovative technologies to improve efficiency and team effectiveness, improve products or services, and continually gain a competitive edge. They do not merely integrate these technologies to stay up with the latest revision; they determine how it will impact the brand and how it will improve overall communication and service to their community of customers.

Knowledge | Visionary leaders create a culture of continuous learning and improvement. They realize a brand is only as good as its team. Investing in knowledge-building creates a sense of meaning for team members and builds a competitive edge and loyalty. Daily focused time around continual learning provides new insights for Visionary leaders and builds a foundation of knowledge that sets them apart from their peers.

Financial Sustainability | Future success is often tied to financial sustainability. Visionary leaders manage finances carefully and with foresight, ensuring the brand has the resources to invest in global opportunities, sustain its long-term growth trajectory, and weather any economic uncertainties.

Performance | Visionary leaders look for and expect the best in each brand team member. They know that when a critical link is broken in a chain, it affects the entire success formula. Establishing key performance indicators (KPIs) and assessing the brand's performance against these metrics allows them to track progress and make strategic decisions.

Environmental and Social Responsibility | Visionary leaders are aware of and considerate of their brand's environmental and social responsibility to the world and society. They think about and find ways to improve or minimize the long-term impact of their company's operations on the planet.

Why Vision Matters

In summary, Visionary leaders consider internal and external factors holistically when assessing their brand's future success. They focus on disruptive innovation, adaptability, and a commitment to creating sustainable value over the long term.

The generational success of a brand is driven first by a Visionary leader's ability to set their vision, second by their effective communication of the reality of the vision, and third by the execution of their vision through others. Any break in this link degrades a leader's ability to achieve their vision.

Vision is widely considered the most crucial factor in a leader's success within a brand or company. Most companies fail for one simple reason: they cannot anticipate what their customers need (as opposed to what they want). As Henry Ford famously said before the invention of the automobile, "If I were to ask my customers what they wanted, they would say a faster horse." Customer demand is the lifeblood of a brand or company; it creates demand not through imitation but through adaptable, innovative, and focused vision.

Imagine. Dare. Succeed.

The Visionary | STEVE JOBS

Your work is going to fill a large part of your life, and the only way to be truly satisfied is to do what you believe is great work. And the only way to do great work is to love what you do.
– Steve Jobs

Born on February 24, 1955, in San Francisco, California, Steve Jobs was the iconic entrepreneur, inventor, and co-founder of Apple Inc. His life story marks dramatic setbacks and triumphs, but ultimately, it illustrates the perfect manifestation of how vision is best cultivated and applied.

Jobs co-founded Apple Computer Inc. (now Apple Inc.) with Steve Wozniak and Ronald Wayne in 1976 in his parents' garage. Their first product, the Apple I computer, was a success, leading to the release of the Apple II, which became one of the first commercially successful personal computers.

Over the years, conflicts within the company led to Jobs' ousting from Apple in 1985. Undiscouraged, Jobs founded NeXT Computer, a company focused on creating high-end workstations for the education and business markets. NeXT struggled in the hardware business but succeeded in the software industry, particularly with its NeXTSTEP operating system. In 1986, Jobs acquired the computer graphics division of Lucasfilm Ltd., which would later become Pixar Animation Studios. Under Jobs' leadership, Pixar produced a string of successful animated films, revolutionizing the animation industry.

Meanwhile, Apple faced challenges in the late 1990s stemming from declining sales and a lack of innovation. In 1997, Apple acquired NeXT Computer, bringing Jobs back into the company as CEO. Jobs quickly revitalized Apple's product lineup, introducing iconic products like the iMac, iPod, iPhone, and iPad.

Under Jobs' leadership, Apple became one of the world's most valuable and influential companies, known for its innovative designs and user-friendly products. Jobs was renowned for his perfectionism, attention to detail, and relentless pursuit of excellence.

In 2004, Jobs was diagnosed with pancreatic cancer, but he continued to lead Apple while undergoing treatment. Despite his illness, Jobs remained actively involved in the company's product development and strategic decisions. Steve Jobs passed away on October 5, 2011, at 56. His legacy lives on through Apple's continued success and innovation and his impact on the technology, entertainment, and design industries. Jobs' life story inspires entrepreneurs and innovators worldwide and demonstrates the power of creativity, perseverance, and vision.

Steve Jobs is a Visionary leader for many tangible and intangible reasons, many of which are associated with his co-founding and leading Apple Inc. and other aspects of his professional and personal life.

Jobs' leadership style was visionary, charismatic, transformational, and sometimes overbearing. He had a clear vision of what he wanted to create and how he wanted to change the world, and he communicated it effectively to his followers, customers, and partners. He could inspire and motivate people with his passion, enthusiasm, and confidence. His leadership skills included creativity, innovation, intuition, persuasion, storytelling, and presentation.

Jobs had an unwavering belief in his vision and the potential of Apple's products. His confidence in the success of his ideas was so strong that it influenced the perception of those around him, creating an atmosphere of conviction. He was known for setting seemingly unrealistic goals and timelines. While these goals might have appeared ambitious, they pushed Apple's teams to strive for excellence and achieve outcomes that surpassed industry expectations. (This method of vision application became known as Jobs' reality distortion field or RDF, which is explored in greater depth in Chapter Six.)

Jobs was a master of creating products that were not only functional but also beautiful, elegant, and user-friendly. He was always looking for new ways to improve existing products or to create new ones that would disrupt the market or create new categories. He had a keen intuition for what customers wanted or needed before they knew it themselves, and he was adept at persuading others to join him in his vision or to buy his products. He used storytelling to craft compelling narratives that captured people's attention and emotions. He challenged them to think differently, to pursue excellence, and to embrace innovation. He also empowered them to take risks, experiment, and learn from failures.

Jobs focused on simplicity and elegance in design and believed in eliminating unnecessary complexities and providing users with a straightforward and enjoyable experience. His philosophy is evident in Apple's minimalist product designs and user interfaces. His vision manifested in his passion for creating products that offered a seamless and intuitive user experience. He emphasized the importance of design aesthetics and functionality, leading to the development of products that were not only technologically advanced but also visually appealing and user-friendly.

He always passionately considered the future and was not worried about the past. He had a long-term vision for the future of technology and the role Apple would play in shaping it. He was not solely focused on immediate gains but was driven by a broader perspective on the industry's direction. This long-term vision helped Apple maintain its relevance and influence, making it the most valuable brand on the planet.

Jobs was instrumental in building the Apple brand as a symbol of innovation, quality, and lifestyle. His ability to create a strong brand identity contributed significantly to Apple's success and its capability to connect with consumers on an emotional level. Known for his demanding and perfectionist leadership style, Jobs set high standards for himself and his team. This approach, while challenging, often resulted in the creation of products that exceeded industry norms and raised the bar for competitors. He rejected ideas that did not align with his vision or standards, causing him to occasionally clash with his colleagues, employees, investors, or competitors.

Fearless in taking risks, Jobs always challenged the status quo. He believed in pushing boundaries to stay ahead of the curve, whether entering new markets or removing traditional product features. Jobs' passion for work and charismatic leadership style inspired and motivated those around him. His ability to articulate a compelling vision and instill a sense of purpose in the Apple team played a crucial role in the company's success.

Jobs faced many challenges and criticisms throughout his career. Some were external, such as competition from other companies like IBM, Microsoft, Google, or Samsung, legal battles over patents or trademarks, and the health issues that eventually led to his death in 2011. Some were internal, such as conflicts with his co-founders Steve Wozniak or John Sculley; power struggles within Apple; and personal issues such as his adoption, his relationship with his daughter Lisa, and his spiritual quest.

Yet his success was not due to an absence of setbacks but to success in overcoming them; without fail, he bounced back from failures, such as being ousted from Apple in 1985 or launching unsuccessful products. He adapted to changing market conditions or customer preferences by introducing new products like the iMac, the iPod, the iPhone, and the iPad. He persisted in pursuing his vision despite obstacles or setbacks. He overcame some of these challenges by being resilient, adaptable, and persistent.

Visionary leaders can learn many lessons from Steve Jobs. Some of the most prominent include:

- Have a clear vision of what we want to achieve and why we want to achieve it.
- Communicate our vision effectively and persuasively to others who can help us realize it.
- Inspire and motivate others with our passion, enthusiasm, and confidence.
- Challenge ourselves and others to think differently, to pursue excellence, and to embrace innovation.
- Empower ourselves and others to take risks, experiment, and learn from failures.
- Create products or services that are not only functional but also beautiful, elegant, and user-friendly.
- Anticipate what customers want or need before they even know it themselves.
- Use storytelling and other effective presentation skills to craft compelling narratives that capture people's attention and emotions.
- Be resilient, adaptable, and persistent in facing challenges or difficulties.
- Be humble, reflective, and open-minded in the face of mistakes or criticism.
- Seek feedback and advice from others who can help us improve or grow.

- Listen to different perspectives and opinions that can challenge or enrich our own.

Steve Jobs was a Visionary leader who changed the world with his products and idea. His approach continues to influence leaders and entrepreneurs across all fields. He was also a remarkable person who left a lasting legacy for generations. He showed us what is possible when we follow our dreams, passions, and visions. Jobs' legacy as a technology pioneer and iconic Visionary leader continues to shape how people interact with technology, making him one of the most influential figures in modern computing and consumer electronics history. The central Visionary traits that set Jobs apart from other leaders include his **adaptability, willingness to grow from mistakes, visualization of new ways of living, out-of-the-box thinking**, and **effective communication**.

Jobs (and the other Visionaries studied in this book) exhibited every one of the key 16 Visionary traits laid out in these pages. These characteristics represent an ideal example for anyone who would follow in his footsteps as a leader, and should be cultivated and integrated into your leadership style without fail.

Your time is limited, so don't waste it living someone else's life. Don't be trapped by dogma — which is living with the results of other people's thinking. Don't let the noise of others' opinions drown out your own inner voice. And most important, have the courage to follow your heart and intuition. They somehow already know what you truly want to become. Everything else is secondary.
– Steve Jobs

ACCOMPLISHMENTS

Co-founding Apple Inc. | In 1976, Steve Jobs co-founded Apple Computer Inc. (now Apple Inc.) with Steve Wozniak and Ronald Wayne. Apple's innovative products and designs have played a significant role in shaping the modern technology landscape.

Macintosh Computer | Jobs was instrumental in developing the Macintosh computer, which was introduced in 1984. The Macintosh popularized the graphical user interface and mouse input, making computers more accessible to a broader audience. With the release of the Macintosh, Steve teamed up with marketing firm Chiat Day and film producer Ridley Scott to create the most iconic ad ever created, "1984." The ad would only be shown once, and to this day is widely considered the greatest commercial of all time.

Apple's Renaissance | In the late 1990s, Jobs led Apple's resurgence by introducing the iMac, a sleek and colorful desktop computer. The iMac's design and user-friendly features contributed to Apple's revitalization and marked the beginning of a new era for the company.

iTunes and iPod | Jobs revolutionized the music industry in 2001 with the introduction of iTunes, a digital media player and online store. The launch of the iPod, a portable media player accompanied by iTunes, transformed how people listen to music and paved the way for Apple's dominance in the mobile device market.

iPhone | Perhaps Jobs' most significant achievement was the introduction of the iPhone in 2007. The iPhone redefined the smartphone industry, combining a phone, music player, and internet device into one sleek device with a user-friendly interface. The iPhone's success transformed Apple into one of the world's most valuable and influential companies.

iPad | Jobs unveiled the iPad, a tablet computer, in 2010. The iPad created a new product category, bridging the gap between smartphones and laptops. It became immensely popular, influencing the design and functionality of subsequent tablet devices.

App Store | Under Jobs' leadership, Apple launched the App Store in 2008. The store provided a platform for developers to create and distribute applications for iOS devices. The App Store revolutionized how software is distributed and consumed, leading to a thriving ecosystem of mobile apps.

Pixar Animation Studios | Jobs acquired Pixar Animation Studios in 1986 and played a crucial role in its transformation into a successful animation studio. Pixar produced acclaimed films such as *Toy Story*, *Finding Nemo*, and *The Incredibles*, establishing Jobs as a significant figure in the entertainment industry.

Legacy of Design and Innovation | Jobs' emphasis on elegant design, intuitive user interfaces, and seamless hardware and software integration set a standard for the tech industry. His focus on innovation and attention to detail influenced the development of numerous Apple products and inspired other companies to prioritize user experience and product design.

Now that we have defined a Visionary leader's vision mindset, let's discuss how their mind works, how they multiply their power by inspiring others, and the other aspects of Visionary DNA.

Chapter 2 | The MINDSET

The mind is everything. What you think, you become.

– Buddha

Visionary leaders have an extraordinary ability to tap into the power of their mind and create a powerful, compelling vision for their brand. By utilizing creative ideation techniques, they can bring bold and innovative ideas to reality and defy current mindsets while still considering practicality. How a Visionary leader approaches their idea generation mechanism and applies it to achieving their vision—that's what we call their mindset, another indispensable yet often overlooked facet of every Visionary.

These Visionaries use their minds to create a persuasive vision of what can be, not what is. They can reach into the future and anticipate needs, inspiring their teams with an unshakable faith in that vision and providing a path to achieve it. This leadership approach requires a comprehensive understanding of the brand's foundational principles, values, mission, and goals and a sharp awareness of current dynamics and customers' future desires. With this knowledge, a Visionary leader can craft a passionate, energizing, and motivating purpose, enabling them to unlock the collective creativity and potential of those around them. By injecting an unwavering passion into their ideas and setting clear objectives, they can gain trust and effectively bring their vision to life.

Their mind clearly understands the ongoing challenges and the constant need to disrupt. They deploy a systematic approach to building an ideation engine, assuring the continual flow of never-ending innovation. Their process is driven by an expansive imagination combined with a Visionary mindset that allows them to evaluate each conceptual idea objectively, preserving its original inspiration. After careful evaluation, they construct a vision that captures the essence of what their brand stands for and inspires their team to bring it to reality.

Inspiring trust and confidence in their team, Visionary leaders guide them through every step of the journey as they work together towards a common goal. By leveraging their creativity and problem-solving expertise, these leaders can effectively create the future landscape for their brand.

One of the Visionary leader's strengths lies in their ability to "think outside the box" and develop breakaway product or service concepts that push boundaries and challenge the status quo of the current environment. They are keenly aware of the latest trends and leverage them as a platform for innovation—carefully building their brand's distinctive tone, style, and culture.

Through the clarity of their mind and judgment, Visionary leaders futurecast product concepts. They call upon their vision and insight to bring their dreams into reality, impacting those around them. Embrace your capacity to conceive ambitious visions—you never know where it will lead!

Visionary leaders understand that success lies in achieving a shared, collective vision. To realize this, they invest their energy and imagination into developing a unified understanding that reflects their brand's values and purpose. They are unafraid to use their mind to think and bring distinctive ideas to the brand, embracing risk-taking and disruption as foundational principles.

Visionary leaders provide strong guidance and mentor team members to succeed beyond others' expectations to ensure their vision is achieved. This leadership ensures all individuals have the tools and knowledge to execute the plan effectively and accurately, converting conceptual ideas into a reality.

Using their influential minds, Visionary leaders can shape something remarkable and inspiring. Creative inspiration combined with technical expertise means they can unlock their brand's authentic potential and develop a passionate vision, setting them further apart from their competitors. A Visionary mindset continually finds ways to inspire the brand to new levels of success.

Mindset Is Dynamic

A Visionary leader's mindset is a dynamic force that drives organizations toward success by harnessing the power of creative thinking and strategic execution. To understand their mindset, we explore the mind of a Visionary leader in this chapter, unraveling the wiring of their brain that enables them to conceive, articulate, and realize a powerful vision for their brands or companies. This allows us to see insights into Visionary leaders' mental frameworks and strategies through a fusion of psychological, organizational, and business perspectives. From the foundation of their visionary idea to its eventual implementation and sustainable generational growth, we can understand the intricate weaving of authentic Visionary leadership.

Visionary leadership is a transformative force that has shaped the destiny of numerous successful brands and companies. The Visionary leader's ability to envision the future, articulate a compelling vision, and lead their team toward its realization is a testament to the profound impact of creative thinking and strategic execution. In this exploration, we will navigate the complex landscape of Visionary leadership, examining how these leaders utilize their minds to conceive, develop, and execute a vision that defines the identity and trajectory of their brand or company.

But how does a Visionary leader's mindset bring an idea to fruition to such exceptional effect? Let's take a cue from some of the top Visionaries and follow a vision from inception to application.

The Genesis of a Vision through the Mind

Creative Intuition and Imagination | At the core of Visionary leadership is the capacity for creative mindstorming— that is, a more abstract application of brainstorming, typically undertaken alone rather than in collaboration and using visual thinking strategies. Visionary leaders possess a heightened ability to imagine possibilities beyond the current reality. Their perceptive processing involves generating innovative ideas through imagination and a creative mindset, then communicating with clarity to their brand leaders who execute this vision through their teams.

Emotional Intelligence and Empathy | Visionary leaders are intellectually sharp and emotionally intelligent. They can empathize with the brand leaders' and teams' needs and desires, allowing them to envision solutions to realize its execution. This emotional intelligence mindset of Visionary leaders enhances their ability to understand and connect with others, influencing the creation of a unified vision that addresses immediate concerns and long-term aspirations.

Formulating the Vision

Communicative Mastery | Effectively communicating a vision is as crucial as conceiving it. Visionary leaders possess exceptional communication skills, allowing them to translate complex ideas into a language that resonates with diverse audiences. The art of communication within Visionary leaders is the ability to define strategies and persuasive techniques expressed through their vision with clarity and passionate conviction.

Storytelling and Narrative | Visionary leaders are often clever storytellers, weaving a narrative vision that captivates and inspires. Storytelling in Visionary leadership is critical to how leaders construct narratives that convey the vision and bring a sense of purpose and shared identity among team members.

Strategic Execution

Transformational Leadership | Executing a Visionary idea requires more than a strategic plan; it demands a transformational approach to brand leadership. Visionary leaders inspire and motivate their teams, instilling a shared commitment to the vision. This principle of transformational leadership explores how Visionary leaders cultivate a culture of innovation, resilience, and continuous progress to realize the vision.

Adaptive Decision-Making | The mind of a Visionary leader is continually looking for paths to successfully execute a visionary idea, which often involves navigating through uncertainty and complex scenarios. Visionary leaders' minds have the capacity for adaptive decision-making and adjusting strategies in response to changing circumstances. This decision-making process of Visionary leaders and their ability to make bold yet informed choices inevitably propel their brand toward its vision.

Overcoming Challenges & Continuous Learning

Resilience and Perseverance | Visionary leaders face numerous challenges in realizing a vision. To meet these challenges, built into the DNA of Visionary leaders are the qualities of resilience and perseverance. These leaders navigate setbacks, learn from failures, and maintain an unwavering commitment to their vision in the face of adversity.

Wisdom and Growth Mindset | An essential element of Visionary leaders' formula of success is they embrace acquiring specialized knowledge and adopt a growth mindset. These leaders build a culture of continuous learning, developing specialized knowledge through "on-the-job" training, not just book smarts. Navigating and applying academic and specialized knowledge is key to finding leaders who can successfully lead the brand's next generation. Visionaries use their mentality to proactively encourage failure, embrace risk, reward experimentation and ongoing adaptation as integral components of the journey toward their envisioned future.

Sustainability and Legacy

Embedding Vision in Culture | For a vision to last, it must become ingrained into the brand's bloodline and culture. Visionary leaders inject their vision into the company's bloodline, creating a lasting impact that outlives their legacy.

Mentorship and Succession Planning | Visionary leaders recognize the importance of nurturing the next generation of leaders and the mindset that must be passed along to others. Visionary leaders engage in mentorship and succession planning, ensuring the continuation of the vision beyond their leadership.

Mindset Is the Road Map

The Visionary leader's mind has a unique ability to think beyond the present moment, seeing their brand as part of something much larger. They use their minds to create a bold and expansive vision for their business—realistic and aspirational. Their vision provides a powerful, passionate point that brings people together, uniting them around a shared goal and inspiring them to strive for greatness. Inspiring trust and confidence in their team, Visionary Leaders guide them through every step of the journey as they work together towards a common goal.

By leveraging their creativity and problem-solving skills, these Visionary leaders can effectively create in their minds a new landscape for their brand. They can paint a vivid picture of the future and communicate their ideas clearly and authentically.

Through creative ideation sessions, Visionary leaders can generate bold and innovative ideas that defy the status quo, tapping into the power of their minds and creating a vivid, compelling future for their brand. They evaluate every aspect of the business to identify growth opportunities and develop solutions tailored to their brand's future. Visionary Leaders are detail-oriented and continuously refine their strategies, ensuring maximum efficiency.

Their power lies in their mind's ability to think outside the box and develop groundbreaking concepts that push boundaries and challenge the current way of thinking. They know of the latest trends and leverage them as a foundation for innovation—carefully defining a distinctive voice, tone, and positioning for their brand that immerses their community of followers in a lifestyle they will continually embrace.

The ability to generate and execute an innovative vision sets Visionary Leaders apart. They create a powerful narrative of opportunity that resonates with their team, inspiring them to move forward and move towards successfully realizing a vision to reality. By constantly refining their approach and innovating in pursuit of excellence, Visionary Leaders ensure their brand will continue to thrive through generations.

In the intricate details of Visionary leadership, the mind becomes the epicenter of creativity, strategic thinking, and resilience. Visionary leaders not only dream of a better future but actively mold that future through the power of their minds. As we navigate the realms of creative cognition, strategic execution, and overcoming challenges, it becomes evident that Visionary leadership is a dynamic and multifaceted journey. By understanding the intricacies of Visionary leadership, companies can aspire to cultivate and nurture the minds that will shape their destinies and leave a lasting mark.

Visionary leaders don't just have big dreams; they also know how to make them come to life. They understand that great ideas need to be effectively communicated and strategically implemented to have any real impact. They consider every stakeholder and resource available, ensuring that every decision is made with intention and purpose. They empower others to join them on their journey, creating an atmosphere of possibility and progress.

These leaders can use their minds to create a compelling vision for their brand. They can anticipate future needs, inspire their teams with an unshakable faith in that vision, and provide direction for achieving it. This forward-thinking approach requires a comprehensive understanding of the company's values, mission, and goals, as well as an awareness of the current global dynamics and ongoing customer needs. With this knowledge firmly in hand, Visionary leaders can craft a shared purpose that is energizing and motivating, enabling them to unlock the collective creativity and potential of those around them. By communicating enthusiasm and confidence in their ideas and setting clear expectations, they will gain trust and effectively bring their vision to life.

A Visionary mind is an ability to think beyond the barriers of the present reality, envisioning a future where dreams become real-world achievements. Visionary thinking involves a unique combination of creativity, imagination, strategic foresight, and a deep understanding of the broader world in which they operate. Those blessed with a Visionary mind demonstrate a capacity to see opportunities where others may see challenges or barriers to success, and they possess the drive to transform their visions into reality by cultivating the appropriate mindset.

Why Mindset Matters

The Visionary leader is a pathfinder, guiding their brand toward a brighter future. Their unrelenting pursuit of excellence is an ongoing expectation, encouraging others to reach new aspirational goals. With their influential minds, they can turn mere concepts into tangible reality.

Visionary leaders can efficiently yet empoweringly imagine concepts through clarity of thought and judgment. They effectively call upon their inner strength to bring their dreams into reality, creating a powerful impact on those around them. Embrace your capacity to conceive ambitious visions—you never know where it will lead!

Inspired by the mindset of famous Visionaries, throughout my life, I have always sought to challenge myself, push my boundaries, and explore the unknown. My creative approach has been fueled by a fearless imagination that constantly strives to redefine traditional approaches and unlock new possibilities.

It's about moving from Idea to Reality even though NO one thinks it is possible.

Think. Visualize. Believe.

The Visionary | ALBERT EINSTEIN

Learn from yesterday, live for today, hope for tomorrow. The important thing is not to stop questioning.
– Albert Einstein

Albert Einstein is considered a Visionary figure due to his incredible mind, groundbreaking contributions to physics, and impact on how we understand the universe's fundamental laws. Many Visionary characteristics contribute to Einstein's status as one of the world's most famous scientific minds.

Einstein's imagination and creativity are renowned. His vivid imagination and creative mind allowed him to think beyond conventional thinking and boundaries. He could visualize complex scientific concepts, and his thought experiments were crucial in developing his revolutionary theories for decades to come.

Einstein was also known for his independent thinking and willingness to challenge established beliefs. He was not afraid to question the status quo and was willing to go against scientific dogma, as was seen in his rejection of classical physics in favor of his theory of relativity.

Einstein was both intuitive and insightful. He often relied on intuition and insight to guide his scientific inquiries and could refine complex ideas into simple, elegant concepts, leading to insights that transformed our understanding of the physical world.

Eccentricity and nonconformity were traits seen in Einstein over his years. Einstein's eccentric personality and nonconformist approach to life and work set him apart. His unconventional thinking and disregard for traditional academic norms allowed him to approach problems from fresh perspectives, contributing to his Visionary ideas.

Additionally, Einstein's interests extended beyond physics to philosophy, mathematics, and music. His interdisciplinary approach allowed him to connect these unrelated fields, cultivating a more holistic understanding of the world.

He would face numerous challenges and setbacks in his career, but his persistence and determination were key to his success. He continued to pursue his ideas despite initial resistance and skepticism from the scientific community. Einstein's vision extended beyond the realm of physics. He was an advocate for peace, civil rights, and social justice. His commitment to using scientific knowledge for the betterment of humanity reflects a broader Visionary perspective.

Famously, Einstein believed in the beauty of simplicity and elegance in scientific theories. His famous equation, $E=mc^2$, encapsulates this principle, expressing a profound relationship between energy and mass in a concise and elegant form. Einstein's relativity theories revolutionized physics and profoundly impacted our understanding of space, time, and gravity. The practical applications of his work, such as the development of nuclear energy, showed to the world the transformative potential of his visionary ideas.

Albert Einstein's Visionary characteristics include **imagination, independent thinking, intuition, persistence, a nonconformist mindset, an interdisciplinary approach**, and **a commitment to the betterment of humanity**. The ideas produced by his legendary mindset transformed our understanding of the physical world and left a lasting impact on science, philosophy, and society. His work continues to inspire scientists and researchers to explore the mysteries of the universe.

ACCOMPLISHMENTS

Special Theory of Relativity (1905) | Einstein's special theory of relativity revolutionized the understanding of space and time. It introduced the famous equation $E=mc^2$, expressing the equivalence of mass (m) and energy (E), with c being the speed of light. This theory laid the groundwork for modern physics and directly impacted nuclear power and quantum mechanics.

General Theory of Relativity (1915) | Building upon the special theory, Einstein formulated the general theory of relativity, which described gravity as the curvature of spacetime caused by mass and energy. General relativity has been confirmed through numerous experiments and observations and remains a foundational theory in modern physics.

Photoelectric Effect (1905) | Einstein explained the photoelectric effect, demonstrating that light can be both a wave and a particle (photon). His work on the photoelectric effect provided strong evidence for the quantization of light and was essential in developing quantum mechanics.

Brownian Motion (1905) | Einstein's analysis of Brownian motion provided further evidence for the existence of atoms and molecules. He showed that the erratic movement of particles suspended in a fluid is caused by the constant bombardment of molecules, supporting the atomic theory.

Mass–Energy Equivalence (1905) | As part of his special theory of relativity, Einstein derived the mass–energy equivalence principle, which states that mass and energy are interchangeable. This equation has had profound implications in nuclear physics and led to the development of nuclear energy.

Einstein Field Equations (1915) | Einstein formulated the Einstein field equations, a set of ten interrelated differential equations that describe the fundamental interaction of gravitation due to spacetime being curved by matter and energy. These equations are the foundation of general relativity.

Quantum Theory of Light (1924) | Einstein's work on the quantum theory of light contributed to the development of quantum mechanics. He proposed that light can be understood as discrete packets of energy, advancing the understanding of wave-particle duality.

Unified Field Theory (Ongoing) | Einstein spent a significant portion of his later life working on a unified field theory, attempting to unify the fundamental forces of electromagnetism and gravity into a single framework. While he failed to develop the theory fully, his efforts paved the way for future research in theoretical physics.

The Visionary | MARIE CURIE

Nothing in life is to be feared, it is only to be understood. Now is the time to understand more, so that we may fear less.
– Marie Curie

Marie Curie, the pioneer physicist and chemist, is considered a Visionary figure in the field of science. Her groundbreaking work in radioactivity revolutionized the understanding of atomic and subatomic particles. Her discoveries, including the elements polonium and radium, laid the foundation for advancements in nuclear physics and chemistry.

Marie Curie faced numerous challenges and discrimination as a woman in the male-dominated scientific community of her time. Despite these ongoing obstacles, she exhibited remarkable persistence and determination in pursuing her scientific research, contributing further to her Visionary leadership.

She is the only individual awarded Nobel Prizes in two scientific fields, a distinction earned by her mindset and accomplishments. Curie received the Nobel Prize in Physics in 1903 (shared with Pierre Curie and Henri Becquerel) for her work on radioactivity and the Nobel Prize in Chemistry in 1911 for her discoveries of radium and polonium. Curie's scientific curiosity and passion for understanding the natural world were evident throughout her career. Her commitment to exploring the unknown and unraveling the mysteries of the physical universe exemplifies visionary thinking.

Marie Curie's work had practical applications beyond pure scientific research. Her discoveries laid the groundwork for advancements in medical treatments, including developing radiation therapy for cancer.

Curie engaged in international collaboration, working with scientists from different countries. Her collaborative approach contributed to the exchange of ideas and the advancement of scientific knowledge globally. Marie Curie recognized the ethical responsibilities associated with scientific discoveries, particularly in radioactivity. She actively advocated for the responsible use of scientific knowledge and its potential impact on society.

It was not incidental that Curie's achievements were even more groundbreaking as a woman in a male-dominated field. She paved the way for future generations of women in science, challenging societal norms and demonstrating that gender should not be a barrier to scientific excellence. Marie Curie was committed to educating and publishing scientific knowledge throughout her years. She actively participated in teaching and mentoring students, emphasizing the importance of advancing scientific education and understanding.

Marie Curie's legacy extends beyond her scientific contributions. Her life and work continue to inspire aspiring scientists, particularly women, to pursue careers in science. The Curie Institute in Paris, named in her honor, remains a prominent center for cancer research. Her many achievements in her lifetime were fueled by a powerful and tightly focused mindset that serves as an inspiration for any Visionary leader.

Marie Curie's Visionary characteristics include her **persistence and determination**, **commitment to education**, **willingness to take on a trailblazing role**, **scientific curiosity**, **practical application of knowledge**, **international collaboration**, and **ethical responsibility**. These traits added up to a lasting legacy that inspires generations of scientists around the world, and her work laid the groundwork for numerous scientific advancements in the 20th and 21st centuries.

ACCOMPLISHMENTS

Discovery of Polonium and Radium | Marie Curie and her husband Pierre Curie discovered the radioactive elements polonium and radium in 1898. This groundbreaking discovery expanded the understanding of elements and their properties and laid the foundation for future research in nuclear physics and chemistry.

Pioneering Research on Radioactivity | Marie Curie conducted extensive research on radioactivity, studying the properties of radioactive materials and their effects. Her meticulous experiments helped establish the concept of radioactivity and its distinction from other forms of radiation.

Isolation of Radium | Marie Curie successfully isolated radium in its pure metallic state, a remarkable achievement given the minute quantities available in natural sources. This achievement demonstrated her expertise in chemistry and solidified the existence of radium as a distinct element.

Development of Mobile Radiography Units | During World War I, Marie Curie and her daughter Irène Joliot-Curie developed mobile radiography units, known as "petites Curies," to provide X-ray services to diagnose injuries in the field. These units played a crucial role in improving medical care for wounded soldiers.

Nobel Prizes | Marie Curie received two Nobel Prizes during her lifetime. In 1903, she shared the Nobel Prize in Physics with Pierre Curie and Henri Becquerel for their work on radioactivity. In 1911, she received the Nobel Prize in Chemistry for discovering radium and polonium and investigating their properties.

First Female Professor at the University of Paris | Marie Curie became the first woman to become a professor at the University of Paris (Sorbonne) in 1906. Despite facing gender discrimination, she continued her research and inspired future generations of female scientists.

Legacy in Medicine | Marie Curie's pioneering work significantly advanced the use of radioactivity in medicine, including radiotherapy for cancer treatment. Her research laid the foundation for developing radiation therapy techniques, saving countless lives in the process.

Chapter 3 | THE IDEAS

Men of lofty genius sometimes accomplish the most when they work least, for their minds are occupied with their ideas and the perfection of their conceptions, to which they afterwards give form.

– Leonardo da Vinci

A unique blend of creativity, strategic thinking, and a future-oriented perspective characterizes a Visionary leader's mindset when thinking about new ideas. Visionary leaders maintain an open mind, actively exploring diverse possibilities and perspectives. They are receptive to unconventional ideas and approaches, understanding that innovation often arises from unexpected sources.

These Visionaries exhibit a natural curiosity, fostering a commitment to continuous learning. They stay informed about industry trends, emerging technologies, and developments in various fields, seeking inspiration for new ideas and embracing imaginative thinking, allowing their minds to wander beyond existing boundaries. They leverage their creativity to envision novel solutions and innovative concepts that can redefine their industry or organization.

Visionaries possess a forward-looking perspective, anticipating future trends and potential disruptions. They consider the long-term implications of their ideas, ensuring that new concepts align with their organization's future goals. A passion for innovation drives these leaders, and they actively seek opportunities to challenge the status quo, introducing groundbreaking ideas that can lead to positive transformation and an understanding that innovation involves risk. They are willing to take calculated risks, recognizing that some failure is inherent in pursuing revolutionary ideas.

Visionary leaders incorporate empathy into their thinking process through ideas that understand the needs and aspirations of various stakeholders. This empathetic understanding helps ensure new ideas address genuine concerns and resonate with their core consumer. Visionary leaders align new ideas with the organization's overarching vision, ensuring that innovative concepts contribute to the long-term strategic goals, providing coherence and synergy within the company.

Visionaries embrace flexibility and adaptability. They recognize that the landscape of business and innovation is dynamic and sustainable with the right pipeline of idea generation. Their ability to adjust thinking and strategies in response to changing conditions is crucial.

Teamwork and collaboration are traits Visionary leaders understand and value. They actively engage with their teams, encouraging a collaborative culture where diverse ideas contribute to the ideation process. Visionaries adopt a holistic approach, considering the connecting points of ideas and their broader impact. They think beyond immediate issues; they focus on the big picture to ensure that new ideas contribute to the company's overall success. Visionary leaders view the generation of ideas as an iterative process. They learn from experiences and continuously refine their thinking, always striving for improvement. Visionaries possess strong communication skills, enabling them to articulate their ideas effectively. They can convey complex concepts clearly and compellingly, gaining the team's trust, support, and clear understanding.

Generating Ideas

A Visionary leader's process for creating unique ideas involves a dynamic and multifaceted approach that integrates creative thinking, strategic vision, and a deep understanding of the context in which they operate. While the creative process can vary from person to person, Visionary leaders often follow a series of principles that enable them to generate and develop unique ideas.

Let's outline a Visionary leader's habits and actions that allow them to create unique ideas, examining how they ensure their Visionary culture is sustainable and carried forward for generations:

Cultivate a Creative Mindset | Visionary leaders maintain an open mind, free from preconceived notions or rigid thinking. They embrace a diversity of ideas and perspectives, and their relentless curiosity drives Visionary leaders to explore new concepts, industries, and emerging trends, providing them with a broad knowledge foundation.

Understand the Landscape | Visionary leaders stay informed about market trends, customer needs, not wants, and emerging technologies. This understanding helps them identify gaps and disruptive opportunities. They conduct in-depth analyses of their industry, competitors, and global trends to gain insights that fuel their creative thinking.

Define a Compelling Vision | Visionary leaders articulate a clear and passionate vision for their brand. This overarching vision is a foundation for generating innovative ideas and disruptive strategies aligning with their long-term goals. Ideas are evaluated based on their alignment with the organization's core brand principles and vision.

Creative Culture | Visionary leaders empower their teams to contribute ideas freely. They create an inclusive and collaborative environment that encourages diverse perspectives.

Reward Innovation | Visionary leaders provide recognition and rewards for innovative ideas among their teams. This helps to motivate and reinforce a culture of creativity.

Think Different | Visionary leaders drive mindstorming sessions where the brand idea generators meet to find ways to disrupt their industry. These idea generators are encouraged to *think differently* and find adaptable products and ideas without fear of judgment.

Embrace Barriers | Visionary leaders view barriers as opportunities for innovation. They drive their teams to find creative solutions within the given limitations. Barriers can drive creativity, motivating leaders and teams to explore unconventional ideas.

Prototype Ideas | Visionary leaders support the creation of prototypes or minimum viable products to test ideas quickly. Refining ideas based on internal feedback and testing is integral to the creative reality process.

Determine Trends | Visionary leaders stay ahead of emerging technologies and trends, exploring how these innovations can be applied and adapted to their product designs or services. Collaboration with tech partners or startups allows Visionary leaders to leverage external expertise and cutting-edge technologies.

Risk Mindset | Visionary leaders are willing to take risks when no one else is willing, understanding that innovation involves venturing into uncharted territory. They see failures as learning opportunities and encourage a culture that embraces experimentation.

Strategic Vision | Unique ideas are evaluated for their immediate impact and alignment with the organization's long-term strategic vision. Visionary leaders assess the feasibility and scalability of ideas to ensure they align with their company's capabilities and growth plans.

Communicate | Visionary leaders must communicate their unique ideas clearly and convincingly to gain buy-in from their teams to execute their vision. They use storytelling techniques to make complex ideas relatable and memorable.

Continual Learning | Visionary leaders maintain a continuous learning mindset, staying curious and adapting their thinking and idea generation based on new information. This acquired knowledge is proactively sought from team members and is used to refine and improve ideas to ensure they can be commercialized. Visionaries nurture a culture of continuous learning, encouraging experimentation and embracing new ideas.

Empowerment | Visionary leaders assemble a team of passionate leaders who are aligned with the vision and have diverse expertise. A strong team is crucial for executing complex ideas. Leaders empower their teams by giving them autonomy to contribute to the execution process. Delegating responsibilities allows team members to take ownership of specific aspects of the vision. They recognize the value of diverse perspectives, creating a culture where different viewpoints contribute to idea generation. These leaders demonstrate transformational leadership, inspiring and motivating their teams to exceed expectations and embrace a disruptive mindset, always challenging the status quo.

Measure | Visionary leaders establish measurable Key Performance Indicators (KPIs) to guide innovative reality. Regularly assessing performance against these indicators provides insights into the effectiveness of the execution strategy. They look for honest, foundational-based feedback from team members and reward those who take risks for long-term rewards. This feedback identifies improvement areas and addresses any challenges that may arise during the execution phase.

Persistence | Challenges are inevitable in any idea-to-reality execution process. Visionary leaders approach challenges as opportunities for problem-solving, leveraging creativity and resilience to overcome obstacles. Persistence is a trait common in all great Visionary leaders and must be a foundational characteristic if you are to succeed where others fail. Visionary leaders demonstrate resilience in facing challenges, viewing setbacks as opportunities to learn and grow.

Legacy | Visionary leaders work to embed their vision into the brand's culture. This ensures that the vision's impact is lasting, far beyond the leader's tenure. Look at Apple; to this day, Steve Jobs' legacy carries on, and his vision has been sustainable. These leaders plan for succession and mentorship to ensure that the next generation of leaders carries forward the vision.

By following these steps, Visionary leaders build a creative and innovative culture, leading to generational ideas that have the potential to transform industries and shape the future of our world.

Why Ideas Matter

Visionary leaders bridge the gap between imagination and reality by seamlessly integrating creativity with strategic thinking, effective communication, and decisive action. They envision ideas and possess the leadership insight to lead their teams toward successfully realizing them, leaving a lasting impact on their companies and industries.

In summary, a Visionary leader's mindset when considering new ideas is characterized by a harmonious blend of creativity, strategic foresight, passion for innovation, and a commitment to continuous improvement. This mindset allows Visionary leaders to conceive groundbreaking ideas and guide their teams in turning them into impactful realities.

Observe. Define. Create.

The Visionary | LEONARDO DA VINCI

Simplicity is the ultimate sophistication.
– Leonardo da Vinci

Leonardo da Vinci is a legendary Visionary due to his extraordinary combination of artistry, scientific, and innovative talents. He is also a perfect example of the power of defining and realizing visionary ideas.

Da Vinci was born on April 15, 1452, in Vinci, Italy. He received no formal education but showed an early ability for art and engineering. Leonardo became an apprentice to the renowned artist Andrea del Verrocchio in Florence. His early works included paintings such as "The Baptism of Christ" and "Annunciation," and he continued honing his craft to create some of his most famous paintings including "The Mona Lisa" and "The Last Supper." His works are known for their meticulous attention to detail, realistic portrayal of subjects, and innovative techniques. Additionally, his use of sfumato (a technique of blending colors and tones) and his mastery of light and shadow not only transformed the art of his time but also set the stage for future artistic developments.

Da Vinci's interests extended beyond art. He was fascinated by anatomy, botany, engineering, and various scientific studies. His detailed anatomical drawings and observations of nature are renowned. With a keen sense of creative imagination and idea generation, da Vinci kept notebooks filled with sketches, ideas, and scientific observations. His notebooks reveal his limitless curiosity and contributions to anatomy, engineering, and physics.

Da Vinci's insatiable curiosity and constant quest for knowledge were central to his visionary nature. He was known for his detailed observations of the natural world, human anatomy, and mechanical devices. As mentioned, his notebooks are filled with sketches, diagrams, and notes reflecting his relentless curiosity about the world around him. Da Vinci's notebook sketches include designs for various machines, inventions, and urban planning ideas. Many of these designs were far ahead of the technology of his era and anticipated advancements that would only become feasible centuries later.

Leonardo da Vinci is often regarded as the archetypal Renaissance man due to his work and ideas, which had a profound and lasting impact on the Renaissance and continue to inspire and influence people across different fields to this day. Da Vinci conceptualized numerous inventions, including designs for flying machines, tanks, and various engineering marvels. While many of these designs were never built during his lifetime, they showcase his Visionary thinking.

Da Vinci's ideas and inventions were only sometimes realized during his lifetime but left a lasting impact on subsequent generations. His notebooks and artworks continue to inspire scientists, artists, and innovators today. He was a true polymath, a multi-disciplined Visionary, excelling in various fields such as painting, sculpture, anatomy, engineering, architecture, and more. His ability to master and integrate knowledge from diverse disciplines allowed him to approach problems and create solutions with a unique and comprehensive perspective.

So what does an aspiring Visionary leader stand to gain by studying this remarkable polymath, especially for someone not working in the world of art? There are three central qualities of da Vinci that are applicable to anyone who wishes to cultivate the idea-generating power of a Visionary:

- **Innovative thinking** | da Vinci conceptualized ideas and inventions far ahead of his time, such as flying machines, armored vehicles, and various engineering projects. His inventive soul was not limited to artistic endeavors but extended to practical applications and technological advancements.
- **Humanism** | da Vinci's fascination with human anatomy and the natural world reflected a human-centered approach to his work. His detailed studies of the human body, both inside and out, contributed to his artistic accuracy and a deeper understanding of anatomy ahead of his time.
- **Interdisciplinarity** | da Vinci saw no separation between art and science. He believed that both disciplines complemented each other and that a holistic approach to understanding the world required integrating artistic and scientific knowledge. This interdisciplinary mindset is the foundation of his Visionary thinking.

Leonardo da Vinci's Visionary nature is characterized by his **exceptional intellect, insatiable curiosity, innovative thinking,** and the **ability to integrate multiple disciplines seamlessly.** His accomplishments continue to inspire and captivate people worldwide, showcasing the depth of his talents and the breadth of his contributions to art, science, and innovation. Da Vinci was a generational Visionary, and his ideas—created and realized through a passion to make the world a better place—impact our lives today and will continue to do so well into the future.

ACCOMPLISHMENTS

The Mona Lisa | Leonardo's painting known as "The Mona Lisa" is one of the world's most famous and iconic artworks. It is renowned for the subject's enigmatic smile and the painting's superb use of sfumato, blending colors and tones to create a soft transition between colors.

The Last Supper | Another of Leonardo's masterpieces is the mural painting "The Last Supper." Housed in the Convent of Santa Maria delle Grazie in Milan, Italy, this artwork depicts the moment Jesus announces that one of his disciples will betray him. The painting is celebrated for its composition and emotional depth.

Vitruvian Man | Leonardo created the Vitruvian Man, a famous drawing that illustrates the ideal proportions of the human body based on the writings of the ancient Roman architect Vitruvius. This drawing symbolizes the intersection of art and science during the Renaissance.

Anatomical Studies | Leonardo conducted extensive studies of human anatomy, dissecting and sketching detailed human body diagrams. Although not widely published during his lifetime, his anatomical drawings were groundbreaking and demonstrated his deep understanding of the human form.

Inventions and Engineering Designs | Leonardo designed numerous machines and devices, ranging from flying machines and parachutes to water pumps and armored vehicles. Although many of his inventions were not built or functional during his time, his sketches and concepts showcased his innovative thinking.

Scientific Observations | Leonardo significantly contributed to various scientific fields, including biology, geology, and astronomy. His observations of nature, such as his study of water flow and rock formations, reflected his scientific curiosity.

Artistic Techniques | Leonardo pioneered techniques such as chiaroscuro (using light and shadow to create a sense of depth) and atmospheric perspective (creating the illusion of depth through color and blurring). His innovations in art greatly influenced subsequent generations of artists.

Notebooks | Leonardo kept extensive notebooks filled with sketches, scientific diagrams, and his thoughts on various subjects. These notebooks have survived over the centuries and provide valuable insights into his creative process and intellectual pursuits.

Chapter 4 | THE PASSION

There is no passion to be found playing small –
in settling for a life that is less than the one you
are capable of living.

– Nelson Mandela

Visionary leaders leverage their passion to drive success in their inventions. Their passion often serves as the origin of inspiration for Visionary leaders when generating ideas, and enthusiasm for a particular field or problem motivates them to explore new ideas and think creatively to find solutions. This inspiration is fundamental in the foundation of groundbreaking work of any kind.

Passion Is Shared

Visionary leaders distinguish themselves not only by the clarity of their vision but also by their passion for sharing that vision so it can be executed. Their ability to inspire, motivate, and instill enthusiasm among their teams is key in turning abstract ideas into tangible reality. Visionaries use storytelling to create a compelling narrative around their vision. They share anecdotes, examples, and metaphors that resonate emotionally, making the vision more relatable and inspiring. Visionaries bring energy and enthusiasm to their interactions. Their passion is visible in their expressions, gestures, and overall demeanor, creating an infectious atmosphere within the organization.

Visionary leaders maintain open lines of communication. They provide regular updates on progress, setbacks, and adjustments to the vision, ensuring transparency and keeping the team engaged. Visionaries align their actions with the organization's values. Their passion for the vision is rooted in a deep commitment to upholding these values, creating a sense of purpose that extends beyond individual ambitions. Visionaries communicate an enduring commitment to the long-term vision. Their passion is not fleeting but sustained, providing a foundation for consistent effort and dedication.

These Visionaries continually and passionately inspire teams by sharing their future vision. This enthusiasm can create a positive and dynamic work environment, cultivating collaboration and dedication among team members. A passionate Visionary leader can rally a team around a shared vision and purpose. They embody the values and work ethic they expect from their teams and actively participate in executing the processes, demonstrating a personal commitment to the vision.

Visionary leaders' passion helps them establish an emotional connection with their teams. They communicate the vision's aspects and emotional and human dimensions, fostering a sense of shared purpose. By infusing passion into executing their vision, Visionary leaders inspire a collective commitment, enthusiasm, and dedication that propels the organization toward its goals. Their ability to make the vision an emotional and motivational force contributes significantly to the success of their endeavors.

Passion also enhances a leader's communication skills. Visionary leaders who are genuinely passionate about their inventions can effectively convey their ideas to diverse audiences, including investors, partners, brands, and communities. Clear and compelling communication is essential for building support and inspiring team members. Passion is contagious; Visionary leaders who radiate passion can inspire and motivate others to join their cause. Visionary leaders communicate their vision with passion and enthusiasm. They use expressive language, inflection, and body language to convey excitement and dedication to their vision.

Visionaries are approachable leaders, and passion feeds that approachability. They create an environment where team members feel comfortable sharing ideas, seeking guidance, and contributing to the vision. This accessibility fosters a collaborative and innovative culture. Visionary leaders celebrate successes with genuine joy. Whether a small achievement or a significant milestone, the celebration reinforces a positive atmosphere and motivates the team to continue their efforts. Visionary leaders invest in the growth and development of their teams. They express passion for the vision and each team member's personal and professional development.

Passion Looks Forward

Visionary leaders immerse themselves in problems yet to be solved, continuously seeking new solutions. This commitment to innovation, disruption, and relentless problem-solving has resulted in the development of revolutionary inventions. Visionaries' strong personal connection to their passion ensures an unwavering commitment to their path to success. This commitment is crucial in seeing an invention through from conception to realization, as it helps leaders stay focused on their goals despite distractions or competing priorities.

Passion often instills a willingness to take risks and explore uncharted territories. Visionary leaders are likelier to experiment with unconventional ideas and approaches, pushing the boundaries of what is known and commonly accepted. This risk-taking mindset can lead to groundbreaking inventions.

Visionary leaders who are passionate about their vision are more likely to engage in continuous learning. Passion drives a thirst for knowledge. They stay up to date with the latest developments in their field and the wider world, integrate new insights into their work, and adapt their inventions based on evolving information. Visionary leaders inspire confidence through their unwavering belief in the vision. Their confidence is contagious, instilling team members with self-confidence and optimism.

Fueled by their passion, Visionary leaders think beyond immediate challenges and envision the long-term impact of their inventions. Passion contributes to the development of a long-term vision. This perspective helps them make strategic decisions that contribute to sustained success. Passion acts as a source of resilience. Visionary leaders often face failures and criticism, but their passion helps them bounce back and continue pursuing their goals while maintaining a positive and resilient attitude in the face of challenges. Their determination to overcome obstacles and learn from setbacks inspires resilience among team members.

In principle, Visionary leaders harness their passion as fuel for creativity, perseverance, and innovation. This emotional connection to their work drives individual success and influences the trajectory of their inventions, shaping the course of technological advancements and societal progress. Passion is what helps Visionary leaders demonstrate unwavering commitment to their long-term vision.

Why Passion Matters

Visionary leaders use passion as a driving force to fuel their success in several ways. Like anyone else in a position of authority, Visionary leaders face numerous challenges in their journey. What distinguishes them is how they overcome those obstacles— passion, an essential motivator that comes from within.

Visionary leaders' passion-fueled motivation helps them persevere through ongoing and continuous challenges and barriers set before them. Passion is the driving force that helps them persist through setbacks, failures, and criticism. It provides the resilience needed to continue refining their inventions. Passion fuels a deep commitment to solving global problems.

Visionary leaders use passion as a powerful force to overcome obstacles, stay committed to their goals, inspire others, think innovatively, and maintain a long-term perspective. Passion becomes the fuel that propels them forward on their journey to success.

Dream. Motivate. Succeed

The Visionary | NIKOLA TESLA

I don't care that they stole my idea... I care that they don't have any of their own.
– Nikola Tesla

Nikola Tesla was a Visionary inventor, engineer, and physicist whose contributions to developing electrical systems and technologies have had a lasting impact on our world.

Tesla was known for his highly innovative and imaginative thinking. He conceptualized ideas and inventions ahead of his time, contributing to the development of alternating current (AC) power systems, radio waves, wireless communication, and numerous other technological advancements. Tesla's work in the field of electricity, particularly his development of AC power systems, revolutionized the generation, transmission, and distribution of electrical energy. His innovations laid the foundation for the modern electrical power industry.

Tesla had a holistic approach to inventions, considering the integration of various technologies into comprehensive systems. His vision extended beyond individual devices to interconnected systems that could revolutionize industries and improve daily life. Among other things, he is remembered as a leading early advocate for wireless communication and transmission of power. His vision included the idea of transmitting electricity wirelessly, a concept that foreshadowed the development of technologies such as radio and Wi-Fi.

Tesla had a global perspective on his work, envisioning the widespread adoption of his inventions and technologies worldwide. Fueled by his passion, Tesla had a vision of providing energy to the world freely and wirelessly. While this vision still has yet to be fully realized, his ideas on wireless power transmission and the concept of tapping into natural energy sources were groundbreaking. His vision for the global impact of his inventions set him apart as a revolutionary thinker and Visionary.

Tesla was known for his independent spirit and determination to pursue his ideas despite financial challenges and lack of widespread support. His independence allowed him to pursue unconventional projects and ideas. Tesla's ideas were often unconventional and went against the fundamental knowledge of his time. While some of his concepts were met with skepticism during his lifetime, many were later proven to be prescient and subsequently formed the basis for significant technological advancements. Tesla's work was grounded in scientific principles, but he often envisioned applications that extended beyond the immediate scientific understanding of his time. His ability to bridge theory and practical application built the foundation for his success.

Nikola Tesla's Visionary characteristics include **innovative thinking, a holistic approach, unconventional ideas, a global perspective**, and **a passion that sustained him through setbacks**, all of which added up to an unparalleled legacy of innovation. Tesla's innovations and ideas continue to influence various fields of science and technology, and he remains a historical generational visionary of electrical engineering and invention. Tesla achieved greatness through his passion for making our world more efficient and communications more effective.

ACCOMPLISHMENTS

Alternating Current (AC) System | Tesla's most significant contribution was developing and promoting AC electrical systems. He designed the AC induction motor and transformer, making it possible to transmit electricity over long distances efficiently. Tesla's AC system is the foundation of the modern electrical power distribution grid.

AC Induction Motor | Tesla's invention of the AC induction motor revolutionized industrial and commercial electricity use. This motor is widely used in various applications, including manufacturing, transportation, and household appliances.

Tesla Coil | Tesla invented the Tesla coil, a resonant transformer circuit that generates high-voltage, low-current, high-frequency alternating-current electricity. The Tesla coil has become a high-voltage symbol and is used in various devices, including radio transmitters and entertainment devices.

Radio Waves and Wireless Communication | Tesla pioneered in understanding radio waves and wireless communication. While he was not credited with the invention of radio (often attributed to Guglielmo Marconi), Tesla's work laid the foundation for wireless communication technologies.

Remote Control | Tesla developed the principles of remote control, demonstrating the first radio-controlled boat in 1898. His work in remote-control technology influenced the development of modern remote-control systems used in various applications.

Wireless Transmission of Energy | Tesla explored the possibility of wireless energy transmission, envisioning a world in which electricity could be transmitted wirelessly, eliminating the need for power lines. While his Wardenclyffe Tower project was never completed, his ideas paved the way for wireless power transmission research in the future.

X-rays | Tesla conducted early experiments with X-rays, producing some of the first X-ray images. His work contributed to the development of X-ray technology used in medical diagnostics.

Robotics | Tesla's concepts and ideas laid the foundation for modern robotics. He envisioned machines that could perform tasks remotely, which inspired future developments in robotics.

Induction Heating | Tesla's work in induction heating led to the development of industrial processes such as metal hardening and cooking appliances like induction stoves, which use magnetic fields to generate heat.

Chapter 5 | The INSIGHT

If one is master of one thing and understands
one thing well, one has at the same time, insight
into and understanding of many things.

– Vincent Van Gogh

Great Visionary leaders leverage insight as a powerful tool to create and lead generational companies. Insight involves a deep understanding of what is needed within their markets, industry, and consumers, which allows these leaders to make informed brand decisions and drive category disruption or innovation.

Visionary leaders have sharp insight into future customer needs and preferences and invest time and resources in understanding their global opportunities, market research, and staying up to date on dynamic consumer needs.

But insight isn't only reactive; Visionary leaders align their insight with a clear purpose. This purpose-driven approach guides decision-making and creates a sense of direction that aligns with their vision. These leaders view failures as learning opportunities and opportunities to analyze setbacks and use them to refine strategies, products, or processes for future success.

As a Visionary leader, your power lies in decoding the future. You don't just observe trends; you dissect them, identifying the DNA of change within recurring patterns. This deep-rooted analysis isn't merely academic—it's your strategic edge. By understanding the trajectory of these trends, you're not just predicting the future; you're positioning your company to shape it. This foresight is what separates market leaders from followers, allowing you to innovate ahead of the curve and dominate your industry before others even see what's coming.

Insight Is Agile

Visionary leaders possess strategic foresight, consider the long-term implications of their decisions, and have a clear vision of where they want to take their company. This insight is both agile and responsive, allowing Visionaries to use their insight to adjust strategies quickly in response to changing conditions or unforeseen obstacles. They also understand the importance of using calculated insights to validate concepts, identify opportunities, and address potential barriers to success. By integrating these insights into their decision-making processes, Visionary leaders not only navigate the complexities of the business landscape but also position their companies for sustained success and growth. Their ability to leverage insight contributes significantly to their strategic vision and the overall impact of their organizations.

Visionary insight is born from a combination of sharp intuition and deep knowledge. While Visionary leaders possess finely-tuned instincts that allow them to perceive connections others might overlook, their insights are also rooted in extensive study and understanding of their business. This blend of innate perception and acquired expertise enables them to anticipate trends and opportunities that elude their competitors. Insightful leaders stay ahead of the industry curve and trends and proactively seek to analyze information about emerging technologies, market shifts, and competitive landscapes, allowing them to anticipate changes and position their companies for generational success. Taking calculated risks is a part of their DNA, the makeup of who they are as a leader; their insight guides them in evaluating potential risks and rewards, helping them make informed decisions that contribute to the company's growth.

Visionary leaders conduct thorough competitor analyses. They identify strengths, weaknesses, opportunities, and threats (SWOT) in the competitive landscape, informing strategic decisions and market positioning. Engaging in scenario planning and creating multiple future scenarios based on different potential outcomes is critical for success. This exercise helps them prepare for various possibilities and develop strategies adaptable to future scenarios. Visionary leaders seek insights from a variety of industries. By understanding how different sectors are evolving, they can identify potential cross-industry innovations and apply them to their own context.

Visionary leaders have a global perspective. They understand the impact of international trends, economic shifts, and geopolitical events on their industry. They adapt their strategies and engage with industry ecosystems, forming strategic partnerships and alliances. This insight-driven collaboration enhances innovation, market reach, and overall competitiveness.

Leaders analyze demographic shifts and changes in consumer behavior. Understanding the evolving demographics helps them anticipate shifts in market demand and tailor their vision to meet future consumer needs. Visionary leaders consider global economic trends, including growth patterns, trade dynamics, and market fluctuations. This macroeconomic awareness informs their vision and strategic planning. Visionary leaders also consider societal and cultural dynamics. They anticipate shifts in values, attitudes, and cultural norms, ensuring that their vision resonates with the evolving mindset of their target demographic.

Insight Is Collaborative

Empowering teams is a key principle of a Visionary leader's success, as well as recognizing the importance of collective intelligence. By communicating openly with their teams, Visionary leaders communicate insights transparently with their teams. This open communication builds trust and ensures everyone understands the rationale behind strategic decisions. They empower their teams to contribute insights and ideas, creating a collaborative environment where everyone's expertise is valued. A collaborative team enhances a leader's insights by providing broader and more current information. This collective intelligence amplifies the leader's vision, offering deeper understanding and real-time data that supplements what an individual could potentially gather alone.

A common tool used by Visionary leaders is **futurecasting**. Also known as futurism or foresight thinking, this method anticipates and shapes future trends, opportunities, and challenges. This proactive approach allows leaders to create a vision that is responsive to the present and anticipates and aligns with future developments.

Visionary leaders closely follow technological advancements and innovations. They assess the potential impact of emerging technologies on their industry and business model, incorporating this understanding into their long-term vision. Through this futurecasting model, they will also incorporate environmental sustainability into their vision. They anticipate growing concerns about environmental issues and integrate sustainable practices into their long-term strategies.

Beyond leveraging their team's expertise and frontline experiences, Visionary leaders collaborate with futurists or experts in foresight thinking. These professionals specialize in analyzing trends and making informed predictions about future developments, providing valuable insights for leaders.

Futurecasting is not a one-time exercise. Visionary leaders continuously refine their vision based on ongoing insights and changes in the external environment and develop agile strategies that can be adjusted based on evolving insights. They understand that adapting is essential in a rapidly changing landscape.

Why Insight Matters

Visionary leaders harness their insights through futurecasting and other forward-thinking practices. This approach enables them to be proactive rather than reactive, crafting a vision that's relevant today, resilient, and adaptable to tomorrow's uncertainties. This forward-thinking approach isn't just one approach; it's the cornerstone of transformative leadership. It's what separates Visionaries from managers, market leaders from followers.

By anticipating change rather than reacting to it, you don't just safeguard your organization's future—you shape it. This is how you build legacies, not just companies. These leaders cultivate empathy for their customers, actively seeking customer feedback and using it to refine products, services, and overall customer experiences. They recognize the value of diverse perspectives and ideas, encouraging idea generation to understand insights that can drive innovation and foster a culture of creativity within their brands. Visionary leaders pay close attention to customer feedback and behavior. By understanding changing preferences and expectations, they can align their company with evolving consumer needs.

Predict. Refine. Execute.

The Visionary | SOCRATES

Beware the barrenness of a busy life.
– Socrates

Socrates, a Greek philosopher who lived in Athens in the 5th century BCE, is known for his insightful wisdom and Socratic method of questioning, which involved asking probing questions to stimulate critical thinking and draw out deeper insights. While he did not write down his teachings, his ideas and dialogues were recorded by his students, primarily Plato, allowing his insight to live on for centuries to come.

Socrates is best known as a great philosopher for his Socratic method, a cooperative argumentative dialogue that stimulates critical thinking and illuminates ideas. This teaching approach, which involves asking a series of questions to encourage self-discovery and examining one's beliefs, has had a lasting impact on education and the development of intellectual inquiry.

To find meaning and truth, Socrates believed in the power of questioning to stimulate critical thinking. Instead of providing direct answers, he conversed with others to help them explore and refine their ideas. Through carefully crafted questions, he sought to uncover the underlying assumptions, contradictions, or gaps in their reasoning.

Socrates was primarily concerned with ethical questions and the nature of virtue. His philosophical inquiries centered around examining moral character, the pursuit of knowledge, and the development of virtues such as courage, justice, and wisdom. Socrates would use a process called *elenchus*, a method of cross-examination aimed at exposing contradictions and inconsistencies in the beliefs of his conversation partners. Through persistent questioning, he led them to reconsider and refine their views. He was particularly interested in discussions about virtue and moral character. By examining these concepts, he believed individuals could better understand themselves and cultivate an honorable life.

Humility was the cornerstone of Socrates' philosophy; he often claimed ignorance and professed that he knew nothing. Rather than speaking from a position of absolute knowledge, he acknowledged his ignorance and sought to engage others in intellectual discovery. This non-dogmatic approach to philosophy allowed for open dialogue and the exploration of diverse perspectives. Socrates believed in empowering individuals through learning and self-examination. His emphasis on pursuing knowledge and understanding oneself was a transformative approach to individual development.

In terms of communication with his collaborators, Socrates employed a form of irony known as Socratic irony, in which he pretended ignorance to encourage others to articulate their ideas. This technique not only facilitated deeper discussions but also showcased Socrates' humility and dedication to fostering the intellectual growth of others.

Socrates championed the importance of intellectual freedom and the pursuit of truth, even in the face of societal norms and expectations. His commitment to intellectual autonomy and the quest for knowledge laid the groundwork for the principles of academic freedom.

Socrates didn't just impart knowledge; he demonstrated a commitment to living an examined life. His pursuit of wisdom and virtue served as an example for others. His life and teachings inspired generations of philosophers, including his student Plato, who shaped the course of Western thought and culture. Just as importantly, Socrates demonstrated intellectual courage by challenging his society's dominant beliefs and assumptions. He fearlessly questioned the views of prominent figures in Athenian society, inspiring a spirit of intellectual inquiry and skepticism.

Socrates is admired for his profound impact on philosophy and influential teaching methods. Socrates' ideas and methods profoundly influenced subsequent philosophers, particularly his students Plato and Xenophon. The Socratic method became a cornerstone of philosophical inquiry and continues to be used in modern education. His commitment to challenging assumptions, promoting self-examination, and pursuing knowledge has impacted how we approach learning and exploring ideas.

Socrates is not typically characterized as a Visionary leader in the conventional sense, as he did not personally bring about significant social or political change. However, his influence on philosophy, education, and critical thinking positions him as a Visionary figure in the history of intellectual thought. Socrates' legacy continues to shape how philosophy is practiced and studied today. His emphasis on questioning, moral inquiry, and intellectual humility remains fundamental to studying ethics and philosophy, and his insightful understanding of and response to the society in which he lived can inspire any Visionary leader.

Socrates' Visionary characteristics include his **humility, desire for knowledge and constructive debate, commitment to ethical principles, willingness to challenge the status quo,** and **dedication to collaboration and honest dialogue with those who followed him.** Any would-be Visionary leader would do well to cultivate these same attributes.

ACCOMPLISHMENTS

Socratic Method | Socrates is renowned for his method of questioning, known as the Socratic method. He engaged in philosophical discussions with individuals, probing their beliefs and challenging their assumptions through questions and answers. This method encouraged critical thinking and self-examination and became a fundamental aspect of Western philosophy.

Ethics and Morality | Socrates focused his philosophical inquiries on ethics and moral virtues. He believed in understanding the nature of virtue and living an honorable life. He famously stated that "an unexamined life is not worth living," emphasizing the importance of self-reflection and moral introspection.

Intellectual Humility | Socrates' approach to philosophy was characterized by intellectual humility. Despite being considered one of the wisest men in Athens by the Oracle of Delphi, Socrates believed he knew very little. This humility led him to constantly question and seek knowledge, setting an example for future philosophers.

Challenging Authority | Socrates challenged Athenian society's traditional beliefs and values, including the authority of the gods and the state. He questioned societal norms and encouraged his students to think critically about the established order, ultimately leading to his trial and execution in 399 BCE.

Influence on Western Philosophy | Socrates' ideas and teachings, as recorded by his student Plato and others, profoundly influenced the development of Western philosophy. His emphasis on questioning, critical thinking, and moral examination laid the foundation for philosophical review in subsequent centuries.

Philosophical School Inspiration | Socrates' approach to philosophy inspired the founding of philosophical schools, such as the Stoics and the Skeptics, whose members valued self-examination and the pursuit of wisdom. His influence extended to various philosophical traditions and schools of thought.

Historic Legacy | Socrates' life, teachings, and trial are documented in the works of his contemporaries, including Plato, Xenophon, and Aristophanes. These writings provide valuable insights into the intellectual climate of ancient Athens and the philosophical challenges individuals who dared to question conventional wisdom faced.

Chapter 6 | THE REALITY DISTORTION

In his presence, reality is malleable. He can
convince anyone of practically anything.
– Andy Hertzfeld, Macintosh team member

The term "reality distortion field" (RDF) is associated with
Steve Jobs, co-founder of Apple. The RDF refers to a Visionary
leader's ability to influence and inspire others by creating a
perception that differs from conventional reality. Visionary
leaders use reality distortion as a tool for positive reinforcement
and motivation. By emphasizing the positive aspects of a vision
and downplaying potential challenges, they "think different" and
define ideas considered outside the box by our current world's
mindset.

Leaders who utilize RDF excel at reframing challenges.
Instead of seeing obstacles as insurmountable roadblocks, they
view them as opportunities to innovate, learn, and create solutions
others may have yet to consider. Visionaries question the status
quo and challenge conventional thinking. They will challenge
conventional thinking and push boundaries, and use reality

distortion to encourage team members, inspiring them to achieve ambitious goals and think beyond existing limitations to consider possibilities that others may find impossible. This leads to building confidence by conveying a strong belief in the feasibility of their vision; even in the face of skepticism, their goal is to rally support and create momentum. By doing so, Visionaries introduce fresh perspectives and ideas that can reshape markets, industries, or even the course of history.

Reality Distortion Is Risky

Embracing risk is a critical foundational characteristic of Visionary leaders when they use reality distortion to encourage failure through risk and achieve innovations through experimentation. A culture that embraces revolutionary ideas creates an environment beneficial to breakthroughs and disruptive innovation.

Visionary leaders create a culture of innovation and cultivate an entrepreneurial mindset throughout their companies. They empower employees to think like entrepreneurs, encouraging them to take ownership of their work and contribute ideas that can drive the business forward. They encourage experimentation, embrace calculated risk-taking, and provide a supportive environment for employees to explore new ideas without fear of failure. Visionaries set aspirational goals that inspire both themselves and their teams. These goals often exceed what may seem achievable in the short term, pushing individuals to think big and stretch their capabilities.

Visionaries embrace an unwavering commitment to their vision, which may involve downplaying obstacles or challenges to maintain focus on the goal, instilling a sense of determination in the team, and shaping external perceptions, such as those of customers, investors, or the media. Strategic silence can be a powerful tool in your arsenal as a leader. While your team values open communication, there are times when discretion is the better part of valor. Used sensibly and ethically, this approach can shape positive perceptions and gain support for your vision. The key is balance: know when transparency builds trust and when temporary confidentiality serves a greater purpose. Master this, and you'll maintain team confidence and gain a tactical edge in executing your strategies. Remember, it's not about withholding—it's about timing your vision for maximum impact and long-term benefit.

Leaders must balance the need for inspiration with a commitment to truthfulness, avoiding intentional deception. They exhibit resilience in the face of setbacks. Instead of being discouraged by challenges, they view them as part of the journey and use setbacks as opportunities to learn and iterate. If reality distortion involves overpromising without a realistic execution plan, it could lead to disappointment and a loss of trust when expectations aren't met. A relentless reality distortion field can sometimes hinder open communication and lead to a lack of transparency. Over time, Visionaries must use reality distortion strategically or face credibility challenges if their promises consistently fall short or the gap between perception and reality becomes too vast.

Rather than focusing on deception or unrealistic aspirations, Visionary leaders can use the RDF strategy to create a compelling narrative around their ideas. During ideation sessions, they enthusiastically communicate their vision and conviction to inspire passion among team members. This environment encourages team members to question existing reality and think outside the box, challenging the status quo and pushing boundaries to explore unconventional solutions.

RDF helps leaders continually and relentlessly establish disruptive goals, entrench a mindset that embraces stretching beyond perceived limitations, and create a culture that values innovation and risk-taking. Visionary leaders must embrace a culture where team members feel empowered to share bold ideas and instill confidence in the team's ability to overcome challenges.

When RDF is used, these leaders highlight past successes and use them as examples to build confidence in achieving new, ambitious goals and master the art of persuasive communication to convey ideas convincingly. They use storytelling techniques to make concepts more relatable and memorable. Leaders must strongly believe in the vision through RDF actions and decisions, showing persistence and resilience in the face of skepticism or challenges.

Why Reality Distortion Matters

In bending reality to succeed, Visionary leaders combine imagination, strategic thinking, adaptability, and a commitment to continuous innovation. By challenging conventional norms and inspiring others to see possibilities where others may not, they contribute to transformative change within their industries and beyond.

It must be restated that Visionaries use reality distortion to inspire and motivate, but they must exercise caution to balance inspiration and openness. The successful application of reality distortion hinges on the leader's ability to align their vision with a realistic path to execution and to navigate the ethical considerations associated with shaping perceptions.

Transform. Reinvent. Revolutionize.

The Visionary | HENRY FORD

Think you can, think you can't; either way you are right.
– Henry Ford

While the concept of the reality distortion field was devised many decades after Henry Ford's remarkable life and monumental work, we can look at his achievements as a model of reality distortion applied with a masterful hand. Ford was known for his unwavering determination, visionary thinking, and ability to shape circumstances to align with his objectives—in other words, using the RDF in all but name.

Henry Ford (July 30, 1863 – April 7, 1947) was an American business icon who revolutionized the automotive industry by introducing assembly-line production techniques and making automobiles affordable and available worldwide. He founded the

Ford Motor Company and was pivotal in commercializing the automobile in the early 20th century. His success can be attributed to his Visionary approach, innovative thinking, and commitment to making automobiles accessible.

Ford was born on a farm near Dearborn, Michigan, in 1863. He grew up in a rural setting and showed an early interest in machinery and mechanics. His early career included working as an engineer and inventor. He founded the Detroit Automobile Company in 1899, eventually becoming the Henry Ford Company. However, he left the company and founded the Ford Motor Company in 1903 with a group of investors. This was an audacious move, and one that would have foundered had Ford not possessed the commitment to shape reality to his vision, building a new world in which mass-produced cars were an indispensable part of life.

Ford believed in his vision of making automobiles accessible to the masses. This conviction infused his actions and communications, instilling confidence in his teams and investors. His unwavering commitment to this vision may be seen as a form of bending reality to align with his goals. In 1908, Ford introduced the Model T, a reliable, efficient, and affordable automobile. The Model T became enormously popular, making car ownership accessible to the middle class. The Model T was a manifestation of Ford's vision.

Ford's vision went against the prevailing norms of his time. At a time when cars were considered impractical luxury items, Ford envisioned a reality where automobiles were practical and affordable for the average person. By challenging the existing reality of the auto industry, he played a pivotal role in revolutionizing it.

Ford's introduction of mass production techniques radically departed from traditional manufacturing methods. By creating an assembly line and standardizing production processes, he transformed the reality of automobile manufacturing, making it more efficient and cost-effective. Ford continually sought innovative ways to improve production efficiency. He implemented conveyor belt systems, interchangeable parts, and division of labor, creating a highly efficient and cost-effective manufacturing process. He emphasized efficiency and productivity, seeking ways to streamline operations and reduce costs without compromising quality.

Ford was known for setting ambitious goals and timelines. The development and production of the Model T, for example, was a testament to his ability to set targets that, at the time, may have seemed like a distortion of reality. Yet Ford and his team achieved these goals, defying conventional expectations. Ford essentially created a new market reality by making cars affordable and accessible. This wasn't just a business strategy but an insightful shift in how people perceived and accessed transportation. By doing so, he reshaped the reality of mobility for generations to come.

Ford's vision extended beyond just building cars; it involved controlling every aspect of the production process. His push for vertical integration, in which Ford's company owned the entire supply chain, was a departure from the reality of fragmented manufacturing. This allowed for greater control over costs, quality, and production timelines.

A famous example of Ford's use of the reality distortion field can be seen during the creation of the eight-cylinder engine. Ford knew the next generation of cars would need to be faster and more powerful to keep up with the market's demands, so he devised a plan to build the eight-cylinder engine. At the time, conventionally-minded automotive engineers dismissed the ideas as impossible, but Ford was adamant that it was being commercialized. The famous Henry Ford quote shared above is a perfect illustration of the power of reality distortion: conventional minds thought they couldn't make an eight-cylinder engine, so they couldn't; Ford thought he could, so he did, and history was made.

Of course, Henry Ford did not *personally* design the eight-cylinder engine; it resulted from efforts by Ford's engineering and design teams. However, Ford played a crucial role in inspiring and steering the company toward innovation. While Henry Ford may not have produced the technical design of the eight-cylinder engine, his leadership, vision, and commitment to innovation created an environment where the engineering team felt inspired and motivated to develop engines that met the market's evolving needs. Ford's influence was felt in the overall direction and priorities of the company, including the decision to introduce the eight-cylinder engine to the Ford lineup.

Henry Ford retired from the day-to-day operations of Ford Motor Company in 1918 but remained involved in the company's major decisions. His son, Edsel Ford, took over as president. Henry

Ford's influence continued, and he returned to the presidency of his company in 1943 during World War II.

Ford's legacy is one of continuous innovation. By consistently introducing new ideas and technologies, he created a reality where Ford Motor Company was synonymous with automotive innovation. This contributed to the company's long-term success and influence. Further, he created a global market for the Ford Motor Company and reshaped the automotive industry by establishing manufacturing plants in several different countries.

While the term "reality distortion field" may not have been applied to Henry Ford in the same way it has to others, his Visionary thinking, transformative actions, and ability to challenge and reshape existing realities align with the spirit of bending reality to achieve goals. Ford's impact on the automotive industry and industrial practices demonstrates the powerful influence that a determined vision can have in shaping the course of history.

Ford's vision left a lasting legacy of innovation in the automotive industry. His ideas and practices influenced the production of automobiles and manufacturing processes in various industries. His goal of making automobiles affordable and accessible to the general public changed how people lived, worked, and traveled. Henry Ford was instrumental in transforming the automobile from a luxury item to an accessible mode of transportation for millions. Ford's legacy extends beyond the automotive realm, influencing business practices, manufacturing methods, and philanthropy for future generations.

Ford's central Visionary characteristics include his **willingness to innovate, audacious goal-setting, risk-taking, uncompromising efficiency, ethical treatment of his workers,** and **far-reaching vision for new markets.** His Visionary approach continues to be celebrated as a key chapter in industrial and business innovation history, and his implementation of reality distortion to accomplish that vision serves as inspiration to all Visionary leaders.

ACCOMPLISHMENTS

Model T | In 1908, Ford introduced the Model T, a reliable, mass-produced automobile that became the first car widely accessible to the American middle class. The Model T's affordability, durability, and simplicity revolutionized the automotive market.

Manufacturing Innovations | Ford's implementation of the moving assembly line in 1913 transformed manufacturing processes. The assembly line allowed for faster, more efficient production, reducing the time to build a car from over 12 hours to around 90 minutes. This innovation dramatically lowered production costs.

Standardization and Interchangeable Parts | Ford used standardized and interchangeable parts in manufacturing. This approach contributed to the assembly line's efficiency and made repairs and maintenance more straightforward, reducing costs for both the manufacturer and consumers.

Fair Wages | In 1914, Ford implemented the $5-a-day wage for assembly line workers, doubling the prevailing wage. This move was revolutionary and aimed at reducing employee turnover, increasing productivity, and ensuring that Ford's workers could afford the products they were producing, thus expanding the market of possible consumers.

Vertical Integration | Ford adopted a vertical integration strategy, owning and controlling various aspects of the supply chain. This included owning rubber plantations for tires, iron ore mines for steel production, and other resources. Vertical integration allowed Ford to reduce costs and maintain control over production processes.

Global Expansion | Under Ford's leadership, the company expanded globally by establishing manufacturing plants in various countries. This global approach contributed to Ford Motor Company's international growth and success.

Labor Innovations | Ford continuously sought innovations to improve labor efficiency. He experimented with different shifts and work schedules to maximize productivity and reduce idle time in the manufacturing process.

Legacy of Philanthropy | In 1936 Henry Ford established the Ford Foundation, one of the largest and most influential philanthropic organizations globally. The foundation has supported education, healthcare, human rights initiatives, and other areas.

Transportation Revolution | Ford's vision and accomplishments transformed transportation from a luxury reserved for the wealthy to a practical and affordable means of mobility for millions. The automobile became a central fixture in American culture and a symbol of progress and freedom.

Influence on Industrial Practices | Ford's innovations in manufacturing and management practices influenced industrial processes across various sectors. Concepts such as mass production, assembly line techniques, and efficiency-driven management have become central to modern manufacturing.

Chapter 7 | The COMMITMENT

Unless commitment is made, there are only
promises and hopes... but no plans.

– Peter Drucker

Commitment is the foundation upon which Visionary leaders build iconic, generational brands. Visionary leaders possess an unwavering commitment that fuels their relentless pursuit of transforming their dreams into reality. They understand that perseverance and unwavering dedication are the path to greatness, and a commitment to their vision keeps them moving forward, even when doubt and adversity surround them. These leaders draw strength from their firm belief in their vision, knowing it can potentially reshape our world.

Commitment Is Strategic

Visionary leaders often use specific personal strategies to maintain their commitment to realizing their vision. While these strategies may vary among individuals, they regularly visualize the successful realization of their vision. These strategies encompass mental, emotional, physical, and interpersonal phases, contributing to a well-rounded and resilient commitment to pursuing their goals. This mental imagery helps reinforce their commitment by making the end goal more tangible. By combining these strategies, Visionary leaders create a comprehensive approach to staying committed to their vision.

They recognize that commitment is not merely a word but a lifeblood flowing through their veins. Their commitment to their overarching vision ignites their passion, propelling them forward even when doubt continually reminds them of the challenges ahead. These Visionary leaders refuse to be swayed by naysayers or deterred by setbacks, instead choosing to embrace challenges as opportunities for growth.

Visionary leaders understand that commitment extends beyond mere words and is visualized and expressed in actions. They lead by example, setting a standard of excellence that inspires others to follow. They are on the front lines with the team, dedicating themselves to the vision and pouring themselves into every opportunity. Their tireless purpose is a guiding foundation for their teams, reminding them that anything is possible with focus and relentless effort.

These leaders also recognize that commitment is not a finite resource but an ongoing, never-ending quest to be pursued by continuously feeding their vision and purpose. They seek opportunities to expand their knowledge, embrace new experiences, and connect with like-minded individuals. By expanding their horizons, they stay inspired and believe in their vision's transformative power.

Finally, Visionary leaders recognize that commitment is a shared responsibility. They actively seek out and surround themselves with like-minded individuals equally passionate about their vision. This creates a powerful ecosystem of support and accountability that propels them toward realizing their vision.

True Visionaries engage their teams in a collective mission, creating a sense of common purpose that builds a brand culture where everyone is held to the same standard and accountable for their contributions. Understanding that they provide calm through chaos, Visionary leaders cultivate emotional intelligence to understand and manage their own emotions and those of others. This skill helps them navigate interpersonal dynamics, foster collaboration, and sustain commitment.

Commitment Is Continual

In breaking down how these Visionary leaders balance this resolute commitment against achieving their overall vision, they utilize personal framework techniques that allow them to be highly productive and personally accountable for creating a path to successfully realizing their vision. Typically, they will break their vision into smaller, achievable goals to maintain focus and tangibly measure progress. This step-by-step approach provides a roadmap for staying committed.

Visionary leaders employ various personal strategies to stay committed to their vision. These strategies often involve a combination of mindset, habits, and daily practices such as:

Time Management | Effective time management is crucial. Visionary leaders prioritize tasks aligning with their vision, ensuring they allocate sufficient time and resources to move closer to their goals.

Personal Reflection | Regular self-reflection allows Visionary leaders to assess their commitment levels, identify challenges, and adjust their strategies accordingly. This introspection helps them stay aligned with their vision.

Mindfulness Practices | Mindfulness techniques like meditation or deep breathing exercises can help Visionary leaders stay present and focused. These practices contribute to emotional resilience and a clearer mindset.

Learning and Growth Mindset | Embracing a growth mindset encourages Visionary leaders to view challenges as opportunities for learning and improvement. This mindset fosters resilience and a commitment to continuous personal development.

Networking and Mentorship | Building a strong network and seeking mentorship provide Visionary leaders valuable support. Interacting with like-minded individuals and mentors can offer guidance, encouragement, and fresh perspectives, reinforcing their commitment.

Adaptive Decision-Making | Visionary leaders recognize the need for flexibility in their decision-making. Being open to adapting strategies based on feedback and changing circumstances allows them to stay committed while navigating uncertainties.

Continuous Learning | Engaging in a lifelong learning approach helps Visionary leaders stay curious and adaptable.

Whether through reading, attending conferences, or seeking new experiences, the commitment to learning supports the evolution of their vision.

Positive Affirmations | Affirming positive statements about the vision and its achievement can help reinforce commitment. Leaders can bolster their determination and resilience by regularly affirming their belief in the vision.

Celebration | Celebrate the small victories along the path to success. Recognize and reward the progress, lessons learned, and growth experienced. Gratitude fuels a leader's spirit, pushing them forward with renewed passion and determination.

Empowerment | Visionary leaders recognize the importance of delegation and empowering their team. By entrusting responsibilities to capable individuals, leaders can focus on the broader vision while ensuring efficient execution.

Positive Mindset | Cultivating a positive mindset is key to staying committed. Visionary leaders focus on possibilities, embrace challenges as opportunities, and maintain optimism even during difficult times.

Adaptability | Being adaptable is essential. Visionary leaders are open to adjusting their strategies based on feedback and changing circumstances while remaining committed to the core vision.

Values | Visionary leaders adhere to core values that guide their decisions and actions. Staying connected to these values reinforces their commitment and provides a moral compass.

With these guiding principles as part of their DNA, Visionary leaders don't wait for perfect conditions; they take decisive action even when uncertain. By integrating these personal strategies into their daily lives, Visionary leaders create a foundation for sustained commitment to their vision, fostering the resilience and determination needed to overcome challenges and realize their aspirations.

They understand that progress comes from experimentation and iteration and are unafraid to fail, learn, and move forward. These leaders are masters of adaptation and flexibility. They recognize that the path to success is rarely linear and are willing to adjust their approach based on changing circumstances and new insights. Visionary leaders recognize that innovation and progress are often required when venturing into uncharted territories. They embrace uncertainty and calculated risks to challenge the status quo and push boundaries. Their willingness to take calculated risks sets them apart from those who prefer to play it safe.

Visionary leaders possess a clear understanding of their purpose, and they bring about that vision with daily efforts to reinforce their commitment. They then can effectively communicate their vision with an infectious fire, inspiring others to embrace it as their own. This clarity of purpose aligns the team's efforts and creates a shared sense of direction.

Why Commitment Matters

Visionary leaders possess a firm, passionate belief in their vision. They envision a future that defies conventional perceptions and relentlessly pursues its realization. This belief fuels their passion and perseverance, driving them forward despite difficulties that inevitably will come with time.

Visionary leaders understand that commitment is a choice and make it daily. They stay focused on their goal, even when faced with setbacks and distractions and refuse to let obstacles deter them from their path.

Are you ready to join the ranks of Visionary leaders committed to making a difference in the world? Embrace commitment as your guiding principle and let it fuel your journey to greatness!

Visualize. Conceptualize. Realize.

The Visionary | ABRAHAM LINCOLN

You cannot escape the responsibility of tomorrow
by evading it today.
– Abraham Lincoln

Abraham Lincoln, the 16th President of the United States, was historically considered a Visionary leader because of his leadership during a critical period in American history. For his struggles leading up to and through the American Civil War, he is rightly regarded as having served faithfully as the nation's soul, preserving its identity as a unified country committed to freedom for all individuals.

Lincoln was born into this world in 1809 in a log cabin in Hardin County, Kentucky. His family later moved to Indiana and then to Illinois. Lincoln began his political aspirations in the Illinois State Legislature and later served a single term in the

U.S. House of Representatives from 1847 to 1849. Early in his career, Lincoln faced many failures, and with his characteristic commitment to the values of this nation, he would push through barriers and accomplish tremendous things.

Lincoln's ability to learn from setbacks, adapt to new circumstances, and maintain his commitment to preserving the Union played a significant role in his journey to the presidency. Lincoln's life is often cited as an example of how perseverance and determination can lead to remarkable achievements, as is the dedication to moral behavior that led to his apt nickname, "Honest Abe."

Lincoln assumed the presidency shortly before the outbreak of the Civil War in 1861. He navigated the country through its most challenging period, preserving the Union and overseeing a nation divided by the conflict. His leadership style emphasized pragmatism, humility, and a commitment to the principles of democracy—and as the soul of the nation he led, through his actions, that nation maintained its democratic ideals through an existential threat.

Lincoln's steadfast commitment to preserving the Union during the Civil War was central to his vision. His leadership during this tumultuous time aimed to maintain the United States as a single, united nation, even in the face of internal conflict. Lincoln demonstrated pragmatism and flexibility in his approach to governance. While dedicated to his principles, he was willing to adapt and adjust his strategies in response to changing circumstances. This adaptability contributed to his ability to navigate the challenges of the Civil War.

Lincoln assembled a diverse cabinet and sought to include individuals with differing perspectives. As historian Doris Kearns Goodwin described, his ability to bring together a "team of rivals" showcased his commitment to unity and the strength that diversity could bring to his administration. Just as the United States was a country of diverse opinions and principles, so too was the Lincoln administration in every respect.

Lincoln's issuance of the Emancipation Proclamation in 1863 demonstrated his commitment to ending slavery in the United States. While this proclamation did not immediately free all enslaved individuals, it set the stage for the eventual abolition of slavery. It signaled a transformative shift in the nation's moral and political landscape. As seen in this legendary document, Lincoln's vision for the country included a commitment to equality and justice. While his presidency did not fully realize the goal of racial equality, his leadership set the stage for later civil rights advancements, including the 13th Amendment and the eventual struggle for civil rights in the 20th century.

He was a legendary communicator, and Lincoln delivered the Gettysburg Address on November 19, 1863, during the dedication of the Soldiers' National Cemetery in Gettysburg, Pennsylvania. The brief but powerful speech is considered one of the greatest in American history. Lincoln was an eloquent and persuasive communicator. His speeches, including the Gettysburg Address and his second inaugural address, articulated a vision of a nation dedicated to the principles of equality and liberty and served to rededicate this country to the principles on which it was founded. His ability to inspire and unite through words was a hallmark of his leadership.

Abraham Lincoln was assassinated by John Wilkes Booth, a Confederate sympathizer, on April 14, 1865, at Ford's Theatre in Washington, D.C. He died the following day on April 15, 1865. His assassination marked the first assassination of a U.S. president and had a profound impact on the nation.

Although his assassination shortened his leadership of the country's soul, Lincoln had a vision for the reconstruction of the United States after the Civil War that stayed true to the same principles that had guided him throughout his life. He advocated a lenient approach to bringing the Southern states back into the Union and sought to promote healing and reconciliation between the North and the South. Lincoln's ability to maintain a steady and persistent leadership style during one of the nation's most challenging periods contributed to his visionary status. He faced intense pressure and criticism but remained focused on his long-term vision for a reunited and stronger United States.

Abraham Lincoln is remembered as the "Great Emancipator" for his role in the abolition of slavery and as a leader who preserved the Union during a tumultuous period in American history. His legacy continues to be celebrated for his commitment to principles of equality, democracy, and justice. Lincoln's moral leadership was a defining characteristic of his vision. His commitment to principles of justice, liberty, and equality left a lasting legacy, influencing future leaders and shaping the nation's moral consciousness.

For any would-be Visionary leaders looking to draw inspiration from this great figure, Abraham Lincoln's Visionary characteristics include his **effective communication**, **pragmatism**, **inclusivity**, **stewardship of democracy**, **steadfast leadership in crisis**, and **commitment to moral leadership**. His leadership during a pivotal period in American history continues to be studied and admired for its enduring impact. Lincoln's commitment toward preserving the Union, promoting freedom, and fostering national unity have solidified his place as one of America's most revered presidents, and may well have preserved the soul of the nation.

ACCOMPLISHMENTS

Emancipation Proclamation (1863) | Lincoln issued the Emancipation Proclamation during the American Civil War, declaring that all enslaved people in Confederate-held territory were to be set free. While this executive order did not immediately end slavery, it marked a significant step toward the abolition of slavery in the United States and redefined the purpose of the Civil War as not only preserving the Union but also ensuring freedom for all Americans.

Preservation of the Union | Lincoln's leadership during the Civil War was instrumental in preserving the United States as a unified nation. His strategic decisions, including appointing skilled military leaders like Ulysses S. Grant, played a crucial role in the Union's victory over the Confederacy.

Gettysburg Address (1863) | Lincoln delivered the Gettysburg Address at the dedication of the Soldiers' National Cemetery in Gettysburg, Pennsylvania. In this brief but powerful speech, he reaffirmed the principles of liberty and equality and emphasized the importance of national unity. The Gettysburg Address is considered one of the greatest speeches in American history.

Homestead Act (1862) | Lincoln signed the Homestead Act into law, providing 160 acres of public land to settlers for a small fee, provided they improved the land by building homes and farming crops. This act encouraged westward expansion, allowing many Americans to acquire land and establish farms.

Pacific Railway Acts (1862, 1864) | Lincoln signed legislation supporting the construction of the First Transcontinental Railroad. This infrastructure project connected the eastern and western coasts of the United States, providing transportation, trade, and communications across the country.

National Banking System (1863) & the Legal Tender Act (1862) | Lincoln's administration established a national banking system and introduced a uniform national currency. These measures stabilized the economy and provided a framework for modern banking practices in the United States.

Thirteenth Amendment (1865) | Lincoln strongly advocated for the passage of the Thirteenth Amendment to the United States Constitution, which abolished slavery in the country. Congress passed the amendment on January 31, 1865, and ratified it later that year.

Leadership and Legacy | Lincoln's leadership qualities, his ability to communicate effectively, and his commitment to democratic principles have impacted the presidency and the nation as a whole. His legacy continues to inspire leaders around the world.

The Visionary | MICHELANGELO

The greater danger for most of us lies not in setting our aim too high and falling short; but in setting our aim too low, and achieving our mark.
– Michelangelo

Michelangelo Buonarroti was a renowned Italian Renaissance artist and polymath who lived from March 6, 1475, to February 18, 1564. He is widely considered one of the most influential figures in the history of Western art, excelling in artistic disciplines, including sculpture, painting, architecture, and poetry. Michelangelo is regarded as a Visionary for his commitment to excellence, extraordinary artistic contributions, and innovative approach to creativity.

Michelangelo was born in Caprese, a small town in Italy. His family moved to Florence when he was a child, and when they recognized his artistic talent, Michelangelo's father sent him to study under the painter Domenico Ghirlandaio. Ghirlandaio was an accomplished visual artist and a poet, writing numerous sonnets and letters expressing his thoughts on art, philosophy, and the human condition. His poetry is known for its reflective and thoughtful nature.

Internalizing the all-consuming commitment he witnessed while studying under his mentor, Michelangelo grew to master multiple art forms. His ability to excel across diverse artistic disciplines showcased his versatility and innovative spirit. Michelangelo's talents extended beyond the arts; he was a polymath interested in anatomy, engineering, and poetry.

His anatomical studies, including detailed drawings of the human body, demonstrated his curiosity about the natural world. Michelangelo was committed to realism and the accurate representation of the human form. His sculptures demonstrated a clear understanding of anatomy and a commitment to capturing the human experience with unparalleled precision. Beyond physical accuracy, Michelangelo's anatomical works often reflected a deep exploration of the human spirit and emotion. The intensity and expressiveness of his sculptures and paintings expressed a deep understanding of the complexities of the human condition.

Michelangelo gained early recognition for his talent in sculpture. His first major works included the "Pieta," a sculpture of the Virgin Mary holding the body of Jesus, and the famous "David," a colossal marble statue that symbolized civic pride in Florence. One of Michelangelo's most celebrated works, "The Last Judgment," was created on the ceiling of the Sistine Chapel in Vatican City. Commissioned by Pope Julius II, Michelangelo painted a series of frescoes depicting scenes from the Book of Genesis. The masterpiece includes the iconic image of "The Creation of Adam." This monumental fresco transformed the chapel into a visionary masterpiece; moreover, it showcased Michelangelo's mastery of composition, anatomy, and narrative storytelling and is considered one of the most outstanding achievements in Western art.

Michelangelo's visionary artistic talent transcended the conventions of his time. His works, characterized by a sense of greatness, emotional intensity, and anatomical precision, pushed the boundaries of artistic expression in the Renaissance. He designed the dome of St. Peter's Basilica in Rome, which was completed after his death. His work combined classical elements with innovative structural solutions. Michelangelo designed the Laurentian Library in Florence, Italy, a masterpiece of Renaissance architecture. Michelangelo's innovative use of materials, including marble and fresco, showcased his technical mastery. He often experimented with materials to achieve new effects and push the boundaries of artistic expression.

Michelangelo's commitment to his craft was marked by persistence and perseverance. Despite facing challenges and setbacks, he dedicated years to completing monumental projects, demonstrating an unwavering commitment to his artistic vision. He was devoted to achieving artistic excellence in every aspect of his work. His meticulous attention to detail, dedication to perfection, and pursuit of the highest standards set him apart as a Visionary artist.

Michelangelo's impact on the Renaissance and Western art cannot be overstated. His work exemplified the ideals of the Renaissance, emphasizing classical forms, human anatomy, and the expression of emotion. His legacy and influence extend beyond his own time: his work had a profound impact on subsequent artistic movements, influencing the Mannerist and Baroque periods and inspiring generations of artists, art historians, and art enthusiasts worldwide.

In summary, Michelangelo's Visionary characteristics include his **artistic vision, focus on the human spirit, innovative techniques, persistence and perseverance,** and **devotion to excellence.** His mastery of sculpture, painting, and architecture and his exploration of various intellectual pursuits solidified his place as one of history's greatest artists and thinkers. Built by a daily commitment to improving his craft and expressing his artistic vision, Michelangelo's legacy continues to influence Visionaries of all types.

ACCOMPLISHMENTS

Sistine Chapel | Michelangelo's frescoes on the ceiling of the Sistine Chapel in Vatican City are perhaps his most famous work. The ceiling is adorned with intricate paintings depicting scenes from the Book of Genesis, including the iconic creation of Adam in which the hands of God and Adam almost touch. The Sistine Chapel ceiling is considered one of the greatest masterpieces of Western art.

The Last Judgment | Michelangelo also painted the monumental fresco "The Last Judgment" on the Sistine Chapel's altar wall. This powerful artwork depicts Christ's second coming and humanity's final judgment. The painting is known for its dramatic composition and emotional intensity.

David | Michelangelo sculpted the marble statue of David, a masterpiece of Renaissance sculpture. The statue represents the biblical hero David before his battle with Goliath. David is renowned for its exquisite anatomical detail and its portrayal of human strength and determination.

Pieta | Michelangelo created the Pieta, a sculpture depicting the Virgin Mary holding the body of the deceased Christ. Carved from a single block of marble, the Pieta is a sublime example of Michelangelo's skill in capturing human emotion and grace in stone.

The Medici Tombs | Michelangelo designed and sculpted the tomb of Giuliano de' Medici, Duke of Nemours, and his brother Lorenzo, Duke of Urbino, in the Medici Chapels in Florence. These tombs are famous for their intricate sculptures, including allegorical figures representing Dawn and Dusk.

Rondanini Pietà | This is Michelangelo's final sculpture, left incomplete at his death. It depicts the Virgin Mary mourning over the body of Christ. Despite its unfinished state, the sculpture is revered for its raw emotional power and unfinished beauty.

Architecture | Michelangelo was also an accomplished architect. He designed the dome of St. Peter's Basilica in Rome, although the construction was completed after his death based on his original design. He also worked on the construction of the Medici Chapel in Florence.

Poetry and Drawings | In addition to his visual arts, Michelangelo was a creative poet and produced numerous drawings and sketches, often exploring themes of love, art, and the human condition. His poetic works and drawings provide valuable insights into his creative mind.

Chapter 8 | The RELENTLESSNESS

History is a relentless master. It has no present,
only the past rushing into the future. To try to
hold fast is to be swept aside.
                                    – John F. Kennedy

The relentless leader is an inspirational, Visionary figure within companies and organizations that have built an aspirational culture and brand. These Visionary leaders' strong spirit sets the course for a company's rise to becoming a generational success. This type of leader possesses a rare collection of traits that create a transformative intensity within their brand, guiding it towards uncharted levels of ongoing success.

Relentlessness Is Empowering

A relentless leader leads through a passionate belief in the reality of dreams, an individual consumed by an unyielding drive to achieve greatness. This passion is the lifeblood that embodies their every action, fueling their unwavering commitment to excellence. The belief in their brand's mission enables them to overcome obstacles that would overwhelm most mortals.

By embodying these traits, relentless leaders create Visionary organizations that are admired and respected. They cultivate a culture of innovation, excellence, and relentless pursuit of near perfection, inspiring their teams to achieve greatness. Their firm determination and clear vision serve as a path, driving their organizations toward a future filled with endless possibilities.

They possess a limitless hunger for knowledge, constantly seeking new insights and perspectives to fuel their decision-making. With a laser-like focus, they relentlessly explore uncharted territories, embracing uncertainty and risk as stepping stones toward innovation and industry disruption.

Relentless leaders possess an unwavering focus, a laser-like concentration on their goals. They are not easily distracted by the countless diversions that can sidetrack even the most remarkable leaders. Their focus allows them to maintain a clear and concise vision for the company, even during turbulent times.

Sustainable success is imperative, so these relentless leaders are integral to ensuring that this is built into a brand's DNA and allows it to achieve generational success. In our world, it is easy to give up or not even begin in the first place; having a relentless leader at the helm is a rare commodity for a brand. In the generations of business leadership, where visionaries create the future and shape the course for others to follow, these relentless leaders are each unique, each passionate about realizing their vision. These individuals are the architects of extraordinary brands, crafting legacies that transcend time.

Relentlessness Is Shared

This relentless pursuit of excellence is not confined to their own efforts; a shared passion spreads throughout the organization, affecting employees at every level with the same burning desire to succeed. This shared passion creates a culture of innovation and creativity, empowering employees to push the boundaries of possibility and challenge the status quo.

A relentless leader masters communicating the opportunities and challenges ahead, inspiring and motivating their team to superhuman accomplishments. They can articulate their vision in a way that resonates with every team member, creating a sense of shared purpose and igniting the fire in their souls.

However, relentless leaders are more than just captivating communicators; they are perceptive listeners. They understand the importance of gathering feedback from their team and customers and are always willing to pivot their course. Open-mindedness and willingness to learn from mistakes are essential qualities for a Visionary leader.

Above all, relentless leaders possess an unwavering belief in the power of their team. They recognize that their employees' collective talent and creativity are the company's most valuable assets. These leaders have recognized that the collective power of diverse ideas can achieve extraordinary feats. They create an environment in which voices are heard, ideas are developed, and individual contributions are celebrated. A relentless leader sets high standards for performance and quality, encouraging team members to strive for excellence in everything they do.

Their vision is not simply a dream; these leaders communicate it in concrete terms constantly and enthusiastically, igniting passion and commitment in every team member. They create an environment where mediocrity is discouraged, continuous improvement is expected, and milestones are rewarded along the way, acknowledging the team's hard work and dedication. They recognize achievements, reinforcing a culture of appreciation for time and hard work while commercializing ideas into reality. They empower their team members to take risks, to think outside the box, and to challenge conventional wisdom.

A relentless leader sets ambitious yet achievable goals for the team, challenging them to stretch beyond their comfort zones. They inspire team members to push the boundaries of what they believe is possible and achieve greatness. A relentless leader fosters collaboration within the team, encouraging ideation sessions, trust, and respect for each other. They create opportunities for team members to work together towards common goals, leveraging each other's strengths and talents. A relentless leader instills a sense of purpose and meaning in the team's work. They help team members connect their contributions to the broader mission and vision of the organization, inspiring a sense of pride and fulfillment in their work.

Finally, their relentless Visionary leadership is not confined to the walls of their organizations; they are agents of change, inspiring others to dream big. They cultivate a culture of innovation and disruption, where employees feel empowered to take risks, experiment, and push the boundaries of reality. They empathize with their community, intuitively understanding their needs and aspirations. This community approach energizes their relentless pursuit of excellence, driving a vision to create products and services that transform lives and leave a mark on the world.

Relentlessness Is Multifaceted

A relentless leader possesses several key traits that distinguish them in pursuing their goals:

Determination | Relentless leaders are fiercely determined to achieve their goals. They possess an unwavering commitment to success and refuse to be moved by setbacks or challenges.

Leadership | A relentless leader leads by example, embodying the qualities, values, and behaviors they aspire to see in their teams. They demonstrate dedication, work ethic, and resilience in their own actions, inspiring others to find the same passion and commitment.

Resilience | Relentless leaders are resilient in the face of adversity. They bounce back from setbacks, failures, and obstacles with renewed determination and focus.

Grit | Relentless leaders demonstrate grit, perseverance, and tenacity in pursuing their objectives. They are willing to put in the hard work, effort, and dedication required to achieve their goals.

Courage | Relentless leaders exhibit courage in taking bold and decisive action. They are unafraid to step outside their comfort zones, challenge the status quo, and take calculated risks.

Vision Clarity | Relentless leaders have a crystal-clear vision of their goals. They have a profound understanding of the future and can articulate it compellingly, igniting the imagination of those around them. They can communicate their vision with such clarity and passion that it becomes a shared aspiration, a flame of hope that guides the entire brand.

Adaptability | Relentless leaders are adaptable and flexible in their approach. They can pivot, innovate, and adjust their strategies in response to changing circumstances or unexpected challenges.

Focus | Relentless leaders maintain a laser-like focus on their goals and priorities. They avoid distractions and stay committed to their objectives despite competing demands or pressures.

Optimism | Relentless leaders maintain an optimistic outlook, even in challenging situations. They see challenges as opportunities for growth and learning rather than insurmountable obstacles.

Accountability | Relentless leaders hold themselves and others accountable for results. They take ownership of their actions and decisions and expect the same level of accountability from their team members.

Empathy | Relentless leaders demonstrate empathy and understanding towards others. They listen actively, communicate effectively, and foster a supportive and inclusive team environment.

Continuous Learning | Relentless leaders are lifelong learners committed to personal and professional growth. They seek out opportunities for learning, self-improvement, and skill development.

Humility | Relentless leaders are humble and open-minded. They recognize they don't always have all the answers they need and are willing to seek input, feedback, and advice from others.

Inspiration | Relentless leaders inspire and motivate others through their actions, words, and example. They lead by example, embodying the qualities and values they wish to instill in their teams.

Principles | Relentless leaders set principles for themselves and their teams. They demand excellence in everything they do, refusing to settle for mediocrity. This relentless pursuit of their shared vision drives their brand to produce incomparable results, consistently exceeding expectations and leaving a legacy for others to follow.

Relentless leaders possess a crystal-clear vision of what they want to achieve. They have a profound understanding of the future and can articulate it compellingly, igniting the imagination of those around them. They can communicate their vision with such clarity and passion that it becomes a shared aspiration, a foresight that guides the entire organization.

They never give up, never surrender, and never allow setbacks to deter them from their goals. Their determination is contagious, inspiring others to persevere even when the odds seem insurmountable.

Why Relentlessness Matters

A relentless leader realizes Visionary transformation, someone who guides their company toward a future of limitless possibilities. Their unwavering passion, focus, and belief in the eventual execution of their vision is the fuel of their company's relentless pursuit of greatness. In their relentless pursuit of excellence, Visionary leaders create companies that are more than just profit-making entities; they are pillars of innovation, platforms for disruption, and sources of inspiration for future generations.

By allowing their relentlessness to drive them forward, Visionaries leave an enduring mark on the world, shaping industries, transforming lives, and leaving a lasting legacy of progress and prosperity. Above all, relentless Visionary leaders are driven by a profound sense of purpose, believing that their work has a meaningful impact on the world.

Struggle. Overcome. Prosper.

The Visionary | ANDREW CARNEGIE

People who are unable to motivate themselves must be content with mediocrity, no matter how impressive their other talents.
– Andrew Carnegie

Andrew Carnegie was a global industrialist and philanthropist born November 25, 1835, in Dunfermline, Scotland. His life was a journey from a poverty-stricken immigrant to one of the world's richest men, marked by his entrepreneurial spirit, innovation, and commitment to giving back to society.

His father, William Carnegie, was a handloom weaver, and his mother, Margaret Morrison Carnegie, worked as a factory worker. Andrew Carnegie was born into a poor family; growing up in poverty, Carnegie's family struggled to make ends meet early in his life. In 1848, at 13, Carnegie and his family immigrated to the United States, settling in Allegheny, Pennsylvania, where his father found work in a cotton mill. This move was driven by economic hardship and the hope for better opportunities in America.

Carnegie's career in the United States began as a telegraph messenger boy for the Ohio Telegraph Company. Through hard work and determination, he advanced rapidly in the telegraph industry, eventually becoming superintendent of the Pittsburgh division of the Pennsylvania Railroad.

In the 1870s, Carnegie recognized the potential of the growing steel industry and shifted his focus to this trade. He founded the Carnegie Steel Company, eventually becoming one of the world's largest and most profitable steel companies. Under Carnegie's leadership, the Carnegie Steel Company expanded rapidly through acquisitions, mergers, and the construction of new steel mills. By the late 19th century, Carnegie Steel was the dominant force in the American steel industry, producing more steel than all of Great Britain.

Carnegie pioneered the steel industry, implementing innovative practices that revolutionized steel production. He embraced the Bessemer process for steelmaking, which enabled mass production of high-quality steel at lower costs. He also employed vertical integration, owning and controlling all aspects of the steel production process, from raw materials to distribution. This strategy allowed him to streamline operations and maximize efficiency. His willingness to think outside the box and embrace change set him apart as a Visionary leader.

Andrew Carnegie's unique characteristics made him a relentless Visionary leader in the steel industry and many other ventures. These traits enabled him to transform the steel industry, amass great wealth, and leave a lasting legacy of philanthropy and social impact. Carnegie demonstrated entrepreneurial vision by recognizing and seizing opportunities in the steel industry. His ability to foresee the potential for growth and profitability in the expanding rail and infrastructure markets contributed to his success.

Carnegie envisioned what he wanted to achieve in the steel industry. From the beginning, he wanted to become a major player in steel production and ultimately dominate the market. His ambition drove him to pursue this vision relentlessly, even in the face of formidable challenges. He was unafraid to take risks and make bold decisions to pursue his vision. He invested heavily in steel production, often leveraging borrowed capital to fund expansion and acquisition efforts. His willingness to take calculated risks enabled him to seize opportunities and propel his company to success.

Carnegie demonstrated remarkable resilience and persistence in the face of adversity. He encountered numerous setbacks and challenges throughout his career, including labor strikes, economic downturns, and fierce competition. However, he remained steadfast in his determination to achieve his goals, overcoming obstacles with unwavering resolve. Carnegie was adaptable and flexible in his approach to business. He quickly adapted to changing market conditions and technological advancements, allowing his company to stay ahead of the curve. He was not interested in outdated practices or traditions, but embraced innovation and disruption.

Andrew Carnegie was a strategic leader who understood the

importance of long-term planning and execution. He strategically positioned his company for growth through strategic acquisitions, mergers, and investments. His sharp strategic thinking enabled him to anticipate market trends and capitalize on emerging opportunities.

His company's strong attributes included empowering and delegating authority to capable managers and executives. He recognized the importance of surrounding himself with talented individuals and trusting them to execute his vision. By empowering others, he fostered a culture of collaboration and innovation within his organization.

Carnegie retired from business in 1901 after selling the Carnegie Steel Company to J.P. Morgan in one of the largest business transactions of the time. In addition to his achievements in the steel industry, Carnegie's relentless Visionary leadership extended to philanthropy. Carnegie funded the construction of over 2,500 public libraries, known as Carnegie libraries, worldwide. He also supported education, scientific research, and cultural institutions through various charitable foundations. Carnegie's vision for education is notably reflected in his funding of public libraries. He believed that access to knowledge was essential for personal and societal improvement, and his funding led to the construction of thousands of libraries worldwide.

In his later years, Carnegie devoted much of his wealth to charitable efforts. He believed in the "Gospel of Wealth," which argued that the wealthy had a moral obligation to use their fortunes to benefit society. Andrew Carnegie's life exemplifies the American dream of rags-to-riches success and the power of entrepreneurship and philanthropy to effect positive change in the world.

Carnegie's philanthropy extended beyond the borders of the United States; his contributions to causes such as education, peace, and public welfare had a global impact, reflecting his vision for positive change internationally. Carnegie advocated for international peace and diplomacy, and his support for peace initiatives, including establishing the Carnegie Endowment for International Peace, reflected his vision for a world that could resolve conflicts through mutually beneficial cooperation.

Carnegie's legacy as a relentless Visionary leader is evident in his lasting impact on the steel industry and society. His innovative practices revolutionized steel production, while his philanthropic efforts continue to benefit millions of people worldwide. His story inspires generations to come, showcasing the transformative impact one individual can have on society through innovation, hard work, and generosity.

Andrew Carnegie's Visionary characteristics include **innovative business practices**, **entrepreneurial vision**, **philanthropic ideals**, **social responsibility**, **meritocratic values**, and **a global vision for positive societal change**. Carnegie's impact on industry, philanthropy, and education are remembered as a model of Visionary leadership. His legacy as an industrialist and philanthropist continues to be celebrated, particularly for his contributions to education and promoting knowledge, culture, and peace. The ongoing effects of his relentless pursuit of the common good remain an enduring testament to his Visionary status.

ACCOMPLISHMENTS

Carnegie Steel Company | Carnegie built the Carnegie Steel Company, one of the world's largest and most successful steel companies, during the late 19th century. His innovative methods and business strategies, including vertical integration and cost efficiency, played a crucial role in the growth of the American steel industry.

Vertical Integration | Carnegie pioneered the concept of vertical integration, in which a company controls all aspects of production, from raw materials to manufacturing and distribution. By owning iron and coal mines, steel mills, and railroads, he ensured a stable supply of resources and streamlined production processes, making his company highly profitable.

Carnegie Endowment for International Peace | Carnegie established the Carnegie Endowment for International Peace in 1910, a think tank dedicated to advancing the cause of international peace. The organization conducts research and provides policy recommendations on global issues related to peace and security.

Carnegie Mellon University | Carnegie contributed significant funding to the establishment of Carnegie Technical Schools in Pittsburgh, Pennsylvania, which later became Carnegie Mellon University. The university is renowned for its science, engineering, and technology programs and stands as a testament to Carnegie's commitment to education.

Institutional Investment | In addition to libraries and universities, Carnegie supported various educational and cultural institutions, including museums, music halls, and scientific research centers. His contributions enriched the cultural and intellectual landscape of the communities where these institutions were established.

Carnegie Hall | Carnegie donated funds to construct Carnegie Hall, one of the most prestigious concert venues in the world. Since its opening in 1891, Carnegie Hall has hosted countless performances by renowned artists and orchestras, contributing significantly to the cultural heritage of New York City.

Legacy of Philanthropy | After selling his steel company to J.P. Morgan in 1901, Carnegie dedicated much of his wealth to philanthropic causes. He funded the construction of thousands of public libraries, establishing a network of educational institutions across the United States, the United Kingdom, and other countries. These libraries provided free access to knowledge and education, benefiting communities for generations. Carnegie's approach to philanthropy, known as the "Gospel of Wealth," emphasized the moral responsibility of the wealthy to use their fortunes for the greater good of society. His philanthropic initiatives set a precedent for future generations of philanthropists, influencing the field of philanthropy and inspiring others to contribute to charitable causes.

The Visionary | JOHN D. ROCKEFELLER

Don't be afraid to give up the good to go for the great.
– John D. Rockefeller

John D. Rockefeller—born on July 8, 1839, in Richford, New York—was an American icon, industrialist, philanthropist, and one of the wealthiest individuals in recorded history. His life is characterized by his innovative efforts in the oil industry, his business intelligence, and his significant contributions to philanthropy.

John Davison Rockefeller was born into a modest family. His father, William Avery Rockefeller, was a traveling salesman, and his mother, Eliza Davison Rockefeller, was a homemaker. Rockefeller spent his early years in upstate New York, where his family moved frequently. From a young age, Rockefeller showed signs of an entrepreneurial spirit. He started his first business venture at 16, entering into a partnership with a friend to start a small produce brokerage firm. This early experience laid the foundation for his future success as a businessman.

Rockefeller's career took off in the mid-19th century, with the development and growth of the oil industry in the United States. He recognized the potential of the up-and-coming oil business and, in 1863, co-founded the oil refining firm of Andrews, Clark & Company. Rockefeller's business acumen and strategic vision would propel him to prominence in the oil industry. He quickly realized the benefits of vertical integration practiced by fellow industrialist Andrew Carnegie, and began acquiring oil wells, pipelines, refineries, and distribution networks to control all aspects of the oil production process.

In 1870, Rockefeller and his partners formed the Standard Oil Company, which would become one of the world's largest and most powerful corporations. Through aggressive tactics such as price undercutting and strategic alliances, Standard Oil dominated the oil industry, controlling an estimated 90% of oil refining in the United States by the 1880s. Rockefeller demonstrated exceptional business acumen and strategic thinking and played a pivotal role in the growth of the Standard Oil Company, implementing innovative business practices that contributed to the company's dominance in the oil industry. Rockefeller had a relentless focus on efficiency in business operations. He sought to eliminate waste, reduce costs, and increase productivity, contributing to the success and profitability of Standard Oil.

Rockefeller was known for his long-term planning and disciplined approach to business. He foresaw the oil industry's potential and positioned Standard Oil for sustained success through careful planning and execution. Rockefeller was instrumental in expanding the market for refined oil products. By creating a vast network of pipelines, refining facilities, and marketing channels, he contributed to the growth and widespread availability of petroleum products. Rockefeller possessed a clear vision of dominating the oil industry. From the outset, he aimed to establish a vertically integrated monopoly controlling every aspect of the oil production process, from extraction to distribution.

Rockefeller emphasized the importance of quality in the oil industry. By standardizing the refining process and ensuring the consistency of his products, he contributed to Standard Oil's reputation for producing high-quality goods.

Rockefeller implemented innovative pricing strategies to gain a competitive edge. He engaged in practices such as secret rebates and favorable transportation rates, enabling Standard Oil to undercut competitors and establish dominance in the market. He was an effective manager and leader. He built a strong and centralized management structure within Standard Oil, allowing for efficient decision-making and coordination across the company's various divisions.

Despite controversy surrounding his business practices, Rockefeller believed that ethical conduct was essential for long-term success. He aimed to maintain public trust by emphasizing fair competition and high standards within the oil industry.

John D. Rockefeller epitomized relentless Visionary leadership through his strategic vision, innovative thinking, and unwavering determination to build and expand his business empire in the oil industry. Having a long-term perspective and was willing to invest time, resources, and effort into building his empire. He focused on sustainable growth and long-term profitability rather than short-term gains.

Rockefeller innovated in business tactics, employing aggressive horizontal and vertical integration strategies. He acquired competitors, secured railroad discounts, and standardized processes to maximize efficiency and undercut competitors. Rockefeller was a master strategist who meticulously planned and executed his business ventures. He strategically acquired oil refineries, pipelines, and transportation networks to create an integrated system that maximized profits and minimized costs.

Rockefeller was committed to driving efficiency and innovation within his business operations. He invested in research and development, implemented new technologies, and optimized processes to improve productivity and reduce costs.

Rockefeller was fearless in taking calculated risks to achieve his goals. He weathered economic downturns, legal challenges, and public scrutiny while remaining resilient and determined to succeed. Rockefeller demonstrated adaptability and flexibility in response to changing market conditions. He adjusted his strategies and tactics to stay ahead of competitors and capitalize on emerging opportunities.

Rockefeller's relentless Visionary leadership impacted the oil industry, business practices, and philanthropy. His Standard Oil Company revolutionized the oil industry and set the stage for modern corporate management practices. Additionally, his philanthropic efforts continue to benefit society through the institutions and programs he established.

Despite his reputation as a ruthless businessman, Rockefeller was also a committed philanthropist. He recognized the importance of giving back to society, and he established numerous charitable institutions dedicated to education, public health, and scientific research. In his later years, he devoted much of his wealth to philanthropic causes, establishing the Rockefeller Foundation, the University of Chicago, and numerous other educational and medical institutions. His legacy as a philanthropist continues to be felt today through the institutions and programs he established.

John D. Rockefeller's Visionary characteristics include

strategic business acumen, focus on efficiency, **philanthropic vision**, long-term planning, market expansion, effective management, commitment to quality, **ethical approach**, and **a global vision for societal betterment**. Rockefeller's life exemplifies the American dream of success through hard work, determination, and innovation. His contributions to the oil industry and philanthropy have left an indelible mark on society, shaping American history and influencing future generations.

ACCOMPLISHMENTS

Standard Oil | Rockefeller co-founded Standard Oil Company in 1870, which became one of the world's first and largest multinational corporations. Standard Oil dominated the oil industry in the United States, pioneering many practices in the modern corporate structure.

Innovation in Business Practices | Rockefeller was known for his innovative business practices, including vertical integration (controlling all stages of the production process) and horizontal integration (acquiring competing companies). These strategies helped Standard Oil achieve unparalleled efficiency and profitability.

Monopoly and Antitrust Legislation | Standard Oil's dominance in the oil industry led to concerns about monopolistic practices. In 1911, the U.S. Supreme Court ordered Standard Oil's breakup into several smaller companies, marking a landmark case in antitrust legislation. Rockefeller's legacy includes shaping antitrust laws and regulations in the United States.

Philanthropy and Education | Rockefeller became a committed philanthropist After retiring from active business pursuits. He donated a significant portion of his wealth to various charitable causes, including education, public health, and scientific research. He founded the Rockefeller Foundation, supporting global health, education, and sustainable development initiatives. Rockefeller's approach to philanthropy, characterized by strategic giving and addressing the root causes of societal issues, set a precedent for modern philanthropic practices. His emphasis on promoting education, public health, and scientific research laid the foundation for many charitable organizations and initiatives.

Rockefeller University | Rockefeller established the Rockefeller Institute for Medical Research in 1901 (now known as Rockefeller University) to promote scientific research and medical discovery. The institution has significantly contributed to biomedical research and is a leading research university.

Public Health | Rockefeller's philanthropy extended to public health initiatives, including efforts to combat diseases such as malaria and yellow fever. His funding contributed to research, education, and public health programs, positively impacting disease prevention and control.

Rockefeller Center | Rockefeller was instrumental in developing Rockefeller Center, a large complex of commercial buildings in New York City. The center became a hub for business, entertainment, and cultural activities and remains an iconic landmark in the city.

Chapter 9 | THE MACHINE

The human brain is an incredible pattern-
matching machine.

– Jeff Bezos

Visionary leaders are often compared to machines while executing their vision, as they seemingly always find a way to fine-tune the areas that need performance improvements. They possess an uncanny ability to translate their dreams into reality. They leverage precise, machine-like execution to orchestrate their plans with flawless precision.

Much like an engine pushing each cylinder to maximum effectiveness, a Visionary leader must fine-tune the brand engine to drive at top speed, utilizing all the horsepower it can produce. Underperformance is not a strategy for executing a plan with maximum efficiency and effectiveness. As such, the Visionary leader creates a culture where maximized performance is integral to success. Their leadership style embodies a unique blend of imagination and practicality. They envision a future where fearless goals are attainable and an innovative, agile roadmap may be followed to overcome unforeseen barriers.

The Machine Is Precise

Visionary leaders are like architects of the future, orchestrating complex endeavors with the precision of a Swiss watch. They believe in their goals and deeply understand the intricate mechanisms to make aspirations a reality. Their leadership style is characterized by meticulous planning, relentless execution, and a clear focus on outcomes. They harness the power of data, technology, and organizational structures to create a finely tuned machine that drives progress with relentless efficiency.

Like master engineers, these Visionary leaders analyze every detail, ensuring that each component of their plan operates in perfect synchrony. Their approach is similar to a symphony conductor, guiding each instrument within the orchestra to play its part in harmony. They inspire their teams with a shared purpose, empowering them to deliver extraordinary results. They leverage technology to streamline processes, improve efficiency, and eliminate obstacles hindering their progress. Through their focus and relentless execution, these Visionary leaders create an environment where innovation flourishes. They create a culture of continuous improvement, empowering their teams to experiment, adapt, and learn from successes and setbacks.

With machine-like determination, they provide their teams with the tools to succeed, continually adapting to what lies ahead and ensuring the brand stays on course. A leader must understand what is needed to constantly and proactively build a team that can sustain long-term success, bringing reality to their vision and inspiring them to embrace the challenges and complexities accompanying groundbreaking endeavors. They establish clear metrics and milestones, relentlessly tracking progress and making data-driven adjustments to ensure alignment with their strategic vision.

These leaders are not content with grand visions alone; they obsess over the details, ensuring that every step forward is taken with precision. They set clear targets, establish robust systems, and empower their teams to execute with precise discipline. By skillfully blending inspiration with meticulous execution, Visionary leaders transform their dreams into tangible reality, leaving an unforgettable mark on the world.

These Visionary leaders often take inspiration from the precision shown by military leaders on the battlefield. While not every Visionary leader faces life-and-death situations on a daily basis, they can learn from the precise and analytical nature of battlefield strategies and apply them in scenarios such as strategic planning, deployment and tactics, team coordination, timing, resource allocation, expansion, victory, and defeat.

Like some of the great military minds, Visionary leaders deploy various methods and strategies with their competitors to achieve success. These leaders combine strategic vision, tactical expertise, and real leadership to outmaneuver and defeat their competitors and make decisive decisions under pressure, often with limited information. They weigh the risks and benefits of different courses of action and choose the most effective strategies to achieve their objectives.

Visionary leaders who utilize military influence conduct thorough after-action reviews following encounters to evaluate performance, identify lessons learned, and make improvements for future success. They foster a culture of continuous learning and adaptation within their organizations.

Overall, these Visionary leaders combine strategic foresight, tactical expertise, effective leadership, and the judicious use of resources to achieve success on the battlefield. They inspire confidence, motivate their troops, and outmaneuver their adversaries through careful planning, decisive action, and relentless pursuit of victory. This is how the machine operates and generates a way forward to the Visionary's goal.

The Machine Is Strategic

Visionary leaders are machine-like in their decision precision, development of strategy, deployment of resources, and vision of long-term success. Some leadership characteristics that Visionaries use in the design and deployment of their machine include:

Competitive Strategy Planning | Visionary leaders start by developing a clear strategic plan that outlines their vision, goals, and objectives. They break down larger goals into smaller, actionable steps, creating a roadmap for execution.

Precise Decision-Making | Visionary leaders rely on precise data and analytics to baseline and support their decision-making process. They gather and analyze relevant data to identify trends, opportunities, and areas for improvement, enabling them to make informed decisions that align with their vision and goals.

Efficient Resource Allocation | Much like military leadership, Visionary leaders effectively and efficiently deploy resources—time, money, manpower, and more—to maximize a team's performance. They prioritize initiatives and investments based on their potential impact and strategic importance, ensuring that resources are allocated where they can generate the greatest return on investment capital.

Process Optimization | Visionary leaders optimize processes and team workflows to maximize productivity. They streamline operations, eliminate waste, and standardize procedures to create a lean and agile organization that adapts quickly to changing circumstances. They implement workflows, procedures, and protocols like well-oiled machines, enabling seamless team coordination and collaboration.

Technology Integration | Visionary leaders leverage technology to support team effectiveness by automating repetitive tasks, streamlining operations, and improving decision-making. They invest in cutting-edge tools and systems that enhance the brand's efficiency, accuracy, and scalability.

Precise Alignment | Visionary leaders ensure everyone understands the vision, goals, and expectations. They communicate clearly and regularly, providing updates, feedback, and guidance to keep teams aligned and focused on achieving their objectives.

Accountability | Visionary leaders hold themselves and their teams accountable for results. They establish key performance indicators (KPIs) and metrics to measure progress and track performance, providing feedback and support to help individuals and teams succeed.

Continual Improvement | Visionary leaders foster a culture of continuous improvement, encouraging experimentation, learning, and adaptation. They solicit feedback from employees, customers, and stakeholders, using insights to drive innovation and refinement of processes.

Agility | By employing precise, machine-like execution techniques, Visionary leaders can translate their vision into reality, driving progress, innovation, and sustainable growth within their organizations. Visionary leaders exhibit agility and adaptability in response to changing circumstances and market dynamics. They anticipate potential challenges, proactively adjust strategies and plans, and pivot quickly when necessary to stay ahead of the curve and seize emerging opportunities.

Relentless Execution | Visionary leaders are relentlessly committed to excellence in everything they do. They set high standards, demand accountability, and pursue continuous growth and improvement, striving to achieve their vision with unwavering precision and determination.

Why the Machine Matters

Visionary leaders may not always operate with the mechanical precision of machines—we are all only human, after all, and neglecting our human needs and qualities is a quick path to burnout. However, they can embody certain qualities and behaviors that emulate the efficiency, consistency, and precision associated with machine-like execution. By adopting such traits, Visionary leaders can effectively translate their vision into action, driving success and realizing their goals with remarkable precision and efficiency. Analyze. Strategize. Repeat.

The Visionary | ALEXANDER THE GREAT

There is nothing impossible to him who will try.
– Alexander the Great

Alexander the Great—born in 356 BC in Pella, the ancient capital of Macedonia—was one of history's most legendary figures, renowned for his military genius, leadership, and conquests. Alexander's conquests were executed with machine-like precision and are hailed for their operational success today. Many of our current military leaders still use and are inspired by Alexander's genius, and his dedication and efficiency have a great deal to teach any aspiring Visionary.

Alexander was the son of King Philip II of Macedon and Queen Olympias. His early education was overseen by the philosopher Aristotle, who instilled a love for learning and a deep appreciation for Greek culture and philosophy. (Incidentally, Aristotle was a student of Plato, himself a student of Socrates—hard to find a clearer illustration of the lasting impact of Visionary leaders than that!) In 336 BC, at age 20, Alexander ascended to the throne of Macedon following the assassination of his father, King Philip II, and quickly asserted his authority and consolidated his power despite his young age.

Alexander's reign is best known for his ambitious military campaigns aimed to expand the Macedonian Empire and establish Greek influence worldwide. In 334 BC, Alexander launched his first major campaign against the Persian Empire, crossing the Hellespont (modern-day Dardanelles) with an army of around 35,000. He won a series of decisive victories against the Persians, including the battles of Granicus, Issus, and Gaugamela. Over the next decade, Alexander led his army across Asia Minor, Egypt, Persia, and the Indian subcontinent, conquering vast territories and founding numerous cities. His military campaigns are considered some of the most successful in history, earning him the title of "the Great."

Alexander's conquests had a profound and lasting impact on the world. He spread his people's culture, language, and ideas throughout the regions he conquered, a phenomenon known as Hellenization, which blended Greek, Persian, Egyptian, and Indian influences.

In addition to his military conquests, Alexander's reign had a profound cultural and political impact on the regions he conquered. He founded numerous cities, many of which were named Alexandria in his honor, serving as centers of Greek culture and civilization. Alexander's conquests facilitated the spread of Greek language, art, and ideas throughout the eastern Mediterranean.

Alexander died under mysterious circumstances in Babylon in 323 BC after a prolonged illness. The exact cause of his death remains a subject of debate among historians, with theories ranging from illness to assassination. His sudden death sparked a power struggle among his generals, known as the Wars of the Diadochi, as they vied for control of his vast empire. Ultimately, Alexander's empire was divided among his generals, with Ptolemy, Seleucus, Antigonus, and others establishing their dynasties in Egypt, Persia, and Asia Minor.

Almost immediately after his untimely death and for centuries to come, Alexander's life and achievements continue to captivate the imagination of people worldwide. He is remembered as one of history's greatest military leaders, whose conquests reshaped the political and cultural landscape of the ancient world.

Alexander the Great is considered a Visionary military leader for several reasons, as his leadership qualities and strategic innovations revolutionized warfare during his time:

Strategic Vision | Alexander had grand ambitions from an early age, envisioning the creation of a vast empire stretching from Greece to India. Alexander aimed to unify the known world under Macedonian rule and spread Greek culture and civilization. His strategic vision went beyond mere conquest; he sought to establish lasting political and cultural influence over the regions he conquered, fostering a sense of unity and cooperation among diverse peoples.

Tactical Innovations | Alexander was a brilliant military strategist and tactician. Alexander introduced several tactical innovations that revolutionized warfare during his time. He combined the phalanx, a formation of heavily armed infantry, with cavalry and specialized units, creating a flexible and adaptable fighting force. Also, he utilized combined arms tactics, rapid maneuvering, and surprise attacks, which allowed him to outmaneuver and defeat much larger enemy forces, earning him a reputation as a military genius. His ability to adapt to different terrains and circumstances showcased his tactical vision.

Lead from the Front | Alexander led from the front lines, fighting alongside his soldiers and setting a bold example of bravery and determination. His courage and charisma inspired loyalty and devotion among his troops, who were willing to follow him into the most dangerous battles. Alexander's willingness to share the risks with his soldiers earned him their loyalty and admiration, contributing to the cohesion of his military forces.

Adaptability | Alexander demonstrated remarkable adaptability and flexibility in his military campaigns. He could adjust his strategies and tactics based on changing battlefield conditions, terrain, and enemy movements. His ability to improvise and think on his feet allowed him to overcome unforeseen challenges and seize opportunities for victory.

Logistical Mastery | Alexander's logistical expertise was key to his military success. He developed sophisticated supply chains and logistical networks that enabled his army to march thousands of miles across inhospitable terrain and sustain itself in hostile territory. His meticulous planning and organization ensured that his army was well-supplied, well-equipped, and always ready for battle.

Inspiring Leadership | Alexander possessed exceptional leadership qualities that inspired loyalty and devotion among his soldiers. He forged strong personal bonds with his men, earning their trust and respect through courage, charisma, and unwavering commitment to their welfare. His ability to communicate his vision, motivate his troops, and instill a sense of purpose and camaraderie contributed to the cohesion and effectiveness of his army. Alexander could inspire his troops with purpose and loyalty, and through charisma, speeches, and personal example, he motivated soldiers to endure long campaigns and face formidable enemies.

Urban Planning and Infrastructure | Alexander implemented innovative urban planning and infrastructure projects in the cities he founded, such as Alexandria in Egypt. These cities became centers of culture, commerce, and learning, reflecting his forward-looking vision for a united and cosmopolitan empire.

Cultural Integration | One of Alexander's visions was to create a unified empire transcending cultural and ethnic differences. He encouraged the integration of Persian and Macedonian cultures, blending customs and traditions to create a sense of unity among his diverse subjects.

Diplomacy | While known for his military conquests, Alexander also employed strategic diplomacy to solidify his rule. He incorporated local leaders into his administration, fostering collaboration and cooperation.

Legacy and Influence | Alexander's military achievements had a profound and lasting impact on history. His conquests reshaped the political map of the ancient world, laying the foundation for the spread of Greek culture and the rise of the Hellenistic Age. His innovative military tactics and strategic vision inspired future generations of military leaders who studied his campaigns and adopted his warfare principles.

Alexander the Great's Visionary leadership, strategic brilliance, and unparalleled military accomplishments have earned him a place among history's greatest military leaders. His innovative tactics, bold strategies, and enduring legacy inspire admiration and study to this day.

When it comes to Visionary leadership, Alexander the Great's legacy offers a powerful lesson for today's executives. His conquests weren't just about military might; they were a masterclass in strategic efficiency. As a modern leader, your 'empire' is built not by constantly reinventing the wheel, but by ruthlessly optimizing and scaling what works.

Consider this: Are you spending your resources on chasing novelty, or are you leveraging proven success? Alexander's approach teaches us to prioritize efficiency over convention, to replicate triumph rather than pursue unnecessary innovation. This isn't about stagnation—it's about strategic multiplication of success.

Identify your 'Macedonian phalanx'—your core, proven strategy in your organization. Then, like Alexander, deploy it with precision across various 'battlefields' in your market. This approach allows you to:

- Accelerate growth by rapidly scaling proven methods
- Minimize risk by leveraging tested strategies
- Outpace competitors who are caught in the cycle of constant reinvention

Remember, true Visionary leadership isn't always about creating the next breakthrough. Often, it's about recognizing your existing breakthroughs and turning them into a repeatable, unstoppable force in your industry.

Your challenge: Identify your winning formula and focus relentlessly on perfecting and spreading it throughout your organization. This is how you build a successful company and a lasting empire in your field.

Alexander the Great's Visionary characteristics include **ambition**, **leading from the front**, **inspiring leadership**, **curiosity and learning**, **strategic diplomacy**, and **a vision for exploration**. His impact on the ancient world and his ability to envision a united and culturally diverse empire contribute to his recognition as a Visionary leader. While Alexander's methods and legacy remain a topic of historical debate and analysis, his influence on the ancient world and his enduring place in the annals of history cannot be denied.

ACCOMPLISHMENTS

Conquests and Empire | Alexander's most significant accomplishment was his unprecedented military conquests. He created one of the largest empires in the ancient world, stretching from Greece and Egypt to India and encompassing diverse cultures and peoples. His empire facilitated the exchange of ideas, culture, and trade across different regions.

Battle of Issus (333 BCE) | Alexander achieved a remarkable victory despite being outnumbered in this decisive battle against the Persian king Darius III. The battle solidified his reputation as a brilliant military strategist and demonstrated his ability to inspire and lead his troops to victory.

Siege of Tyre (332 BCE) | The successful siege of the island city of Tyre showcased Alexander's determination and engineering skills. He built a causeway to connect the island to the mainland, overcoming significant geographical challenges to capture the city.

Egyptian Campaign and Foundation of Alexandria | Alexander's conquest of Egypt was relatively peaceful, and the Egyptians welcomed him as a liberator. He founded the city of Alexandria, which later became a major center of learning and culture in the ancient world.

Battle of Gaugamela (331 BCE) | This battle against Darius III is often considered one of Alexander's greatest victories. He employed innovative tactics, including a feigned retreat, to defeat the Persian forces decisively. After this battle, the Achaemenid Persian Empire began to crumble.

Cultural Exchange and Hellenization | Alexander's empire became a melting pot of cultures and ideas. He encouraged the exchange of knowledge and customs between different regions, a process known as Hellenization, where Greek culture and language influenced the conquered territories. This cultural diffusion had a lasting impact on the development of art, philosophy, and science in the Hellenistic world.

Patronage of Arts and Sciences | Alexander patronized scholars, philosophers, and scientists, fostering an environment of learning and intellectual curiosity. His support for education and the arts contributed to the flourishing of knowledge in his empire.

Legacy of Military Tactics | Alexander's military strategies and tactics continued to influence military leaders for centuries. His methods, such as the use of combined arms and rapid maneuvering, were studied and emulated by future commanders.

Spread of Greek Language and Culture | Through his conquests and policies, Alexander facilitated the spread of Greek language and culture throughout his empire. This cultural unity laid the foundation for the later Hellenistic period, characterized by Greek cultural influence in Asia and the Middle East.

Mythic Status and Historical Impact | Alexander's life and achievements inspired numerous legends and myths, making him a legendary figure in both Western and Eastern cultures. His conquests profoundly impacted the course of history, shaping the development of civilizations in the centuries that followed.

The Visionary | CLARENCE "KELLY" JOHNSON

If you can't do it with brainpower, you can't do it with manpower.
– Kelly Johnson

Clarence "Kelly" Johnson (1910–1990) was an American aeronautical engineer and a Visionary in aviation. His contributions revolutionized aircraft design and engineering, leading to some of the most iconic and advanced aircraft of the 20th century.

Clarence Leonard Johnson was born on February 27, 1910, in Ishpeming, Michigan. From a young age, he displayed skills in engineering and aviation, building model airplanes and visualizing flight. Johnson attended the University of Michigan, where he studied aeronautical engineering and graduated with a Bachelor of Science in 1932.

In 1933, Johnson joined the Lockheed Aircraft Corporation (later Lockheed Martin) as a tool designer. His talent and innovative ideas quickly caught the attention of company executives. Johnson's career at Lockheed spanned over four decades, during which he played a key role in designing and developing numerous groundbreaking aircraft. Johnson was a highly skilled aircraft designer and engineer. His expertise in aeronautics allowed him to conceptualize and develop advanced aircraft that pushed the boundaries of technology and performance. Johnson was known for his hands-on leadership style. He actively participated in the design and development of aircraft, fostering a collaborative and innovative work environment. His personal involvement contributed to the success of the projects under his leadership.

Johnson understood the importance of secrecy and security in the defense industry. His division operated with a high level of confidentiality to protect sensitive information related to aircraft design and technology. This allowed Johnson's team to work on classified projects with minimal external interference, maintained by a machine-like method of collaboration and innovation.

He is best known for founding and leading Lockheed's Skunk Works division, a secretive and highly innovative research and development facility. Under Johnson's leadership, Skunk Works became synonymous with cutting-edge aerospace technology and engineering excellence. Some of the most iconic aircraft developed by Skunk Works under Johnson's leadership include the P-38 Lightning, the U-2 reconnaissance aircraft, the SR-71 Blackbird, and the F-117 Nighthawk stealth fighter.

Johnson was fearless in taking risks and pushing the boundaries of existing technology. The aircraft developed under his leadership, such as the SR-71 Blackbird, represented cutting-edge aerodynamics, materials, and propulsion innovations. Johnson was known for his unconventional aircraft design approach, prioritizing simplicity, performance, and cost-effectiveness. He pioneered using advanced materials, aerodynamics, and propulsion systems to push the boundaries of aviation technology. Johnson's "rule of seven" design philosophy, which aimed to achieve seven major performance goals for every aircraft project, became a trademark of Skunk Works' engineering methodology.

By leading Lockheed's Skunk Works division, Johnson significantly contributed to military stealth technology. While Johnson did not invent stealth technology, he played a pivotal role in developing stealth aircraft and oversaw several key projects that advanced the field. Johnson and his team at Skunk Works developed advanced stealth techniques and technologies to minimize aircraft's radar cross-section (RCS). This included using faceted surfaces, radar-absorbent materials, and other design features to reduce radar reflections and make aircraft less detectable to enemy radar systems. Beyond the F-117, Johnson continued to support research and development efforts in stealth technology. Under his guidance, Skunk Works explored new concepts and technologies for stealth aircraft, leading to the development of advanced platforms like the B-2 Spirit bomber and the F-22 Raptor fighter jet.

Johnson's mantra was "keep it simple" when it came to aircraft design. He believed in simplicity and efficiency, emphasizing the importance of practical and straightforward solutions to engineering challenges. This approach contributed to the success of Skunk Works projects. Johnson promoted rapid prototyping and iterative testing to accelerate the development process. This approach allowed Skunk Works to quickly design, build, and test new aircraft concepts, reducing development timelines and ensuring adaptability to changing requirements. Like other Visionaries, his machine-like mindset emphasized efficiency and a frictionless path between innovation, development, and production.

Johnson's leadership and aircraft design and engineering expertise were instrumental in shaping stealth technology. His innovative approach to aircraft design and his commitment to excellence and efficiency laid the foundation for developing stealth aircraft that have since become integral to modern military operations.

Johnson had a long-term vision for the future of aviation. He anticipated the need for advanced technologies and capabilities, guiding Skunk Works to develop aircraft ahead of their time and laying the foundation for future generations of aerospace innovation. His contributions to military stealth technology, particularly through his leadership of Lockheed's Skunk Works division, played a crucial role in advancing the field and transforming the capabilities of military aircraft.

Johnson's Visionary leadership and pioneering achievements have made him a legendary figure in the aviation field. His legacy lives on through the groundbreaking aircraft he helped to create and the lasting impact of his innovative engineering principles, which earned him numerous awards and honors throughout his career. He received the National Medal of Science in 1964 and was inducted into the National Aviation Hall of Fame in 1973. His contributions to the aerospace industry and establishing Skunk Works as a center for innovation have inspired subsequent generations of engineers and designers. His innovative spirit, bold vision, and relentless pursuit of excellence have left an indelible mark on the history of aviation.

Kelly Johnson's Visionary characteristics include his **"keep it simple" philosophy**, **rapid prototyping**, **hands-on leadership**, **a commitment to security**, **risk-taking and innovation**, **a focus on performance**, and **long-term vision**. Kelly's far-reaching innovation and machine-like efficiency brought to life a great many critical defense goals for the United States and built his own unquestioned legacy of innovation that continues to influence the aerospace industry.

ACCOMPLISHMENTS

Skunk Works | Johnson established and led Lockheed's Skunk Works, a highly secretive and innovative division within the company. Under his leadership, Skunk Works developed a series of cutting-edge aircraft, many of which became iconic and played pivotal roles in military aviation.

P-38 Lightning | Johnson was one of the chief designers of the Lockheed P-38 Lightning, a versatile and highly successful fighter aircraft used during World War II. The P-38 was known for its distinctive twin-boom design and superior performance, becoming one of the most recognizable fighter planes of the era.

Constellation | Johnson played a key role in the design and development of the Lockheed Constellation, a pioneering civilian airliner that introduced innovations such as pressurized cabins and a triple-tail design. The Constellation revolutionized long-distance air travel and set new standards for comfort and safety.

U-2 Spy Plane | One of Johnson's most famous creations was the U-2 spy plane, a high-altitude reconnaissance aircraft used by the United States Air Force. The U-2 played a crucial role in intelligence gathering during the Cold War, providing valuable information about enemy activities and nuclear capabilities.

SR-71 Blackbird | Johnson led the development of the SR-71 Blackbird, a strategic reconnaissance aircraft renowned for its incredible speed and altitude capabilities. The SR-71 set numerous speed and altitude records and remains one of the fastest aircraft ever built.

Innovations in Aircraft Design | Johnson was known for his innovative approach to aircraft design, incorporating advanced aerodynamics, materials, and propulsion systems into his creations. His emphasis on performance, efficiency, and reliability influenced the design principles of many modern aircraft.

Have Blue Program | One of Johnson's most notable contributions to stealth technology was the development of the Have Blue Program, which aimed to demonstrate the feasibility of stealth aircraft design. Under Johnson's leadership, Skunk Works built and tested two prototype aircraft, known as Have Blue, in the late 1970s.

F117A Nighthawk | The success of the Have Blue Program paved the way for the development of the F-117 Nighthawk, the world's first operational stealth aircraft. Johnson oversaw the design and production of the F-117, unveiled to the public in 1988 and played a prominent role in military operations during the Gulf War.

Advancement of Stealth Technology | Johnson's work on classified projects at Skunk Works laid the foundation for advancements in stealth technology. His team's work on radar-evading aircraft designs contributed to developing stealth bombers and fighters in subsequent decades.

Legacy of Leadership | Johnson's leadership style and emphasis on innovation, efficiency, and precision engineering at Skunk Works established a legacy of excellence in aerospace engineering. His management principles inspire engineers and project managers in the aerospace industry.

Chapter 10 | The RISK

He who is not courageous enough to take risks
will accomplish nothing in life.

— Muhammad Ali

Another principle Visionary leaders embrace is risk-taking, a necessary trait to execute an ongoing vision successfully. Risk-taking is essential to the success of Visionary leaders, who often seek to push the boundaries of what is possible and achieve what some would consider unattainable goals.

Visionary leaders understand that true success lies not in avoiding risks but in embracing them with courage and foresight. They step into unexplored territories with firm determination, driven by curiosity and a relentless pursuit of innovation. Fear— that paralyzing force that holds many captive—becomes their fuel. They harness its energy to propel themselves forward, transforming overwhelming challenges into opportunities for growth and resilience.

Risk-taking allows them to explore new ideas, experiment with unconventional approaches, and innovate in ways that can lead to breakthroughs and advancements. Visionary leaders take risks before achieving success through strategic thinking, calculated decision-making, and a willingness to embrace uncertainty.

Risk is Required

In today's rapidly changing world, playing it safe can lead to stagnation or irrelevance. Visionary leaders understand the importance of adaptability and agility, which often require taking calculated risks to navigate uncertainty and seize opportunities in dynamic environments. Taking strategic risks can give Visionary leaders a competitive advantage by allowing them to differentiate themselves from competitors. Whether it's entering new markets, developing innovative products, or adopting disruptive technologies, risk-taking can position leaders ahead of the curve and drive growth and success.

Embracing risk-taking creates a culture of learning and growth within organizations. Visionary leaders encourage their teams to take risks, learn from mistakes, and iterate to improve outcomes over time. They empower their teams to take ownership of projects, explore new ideas, and challenge the status quo without fear of retaliation for failure. By leading through example and showing that calculated risks are worth taking, leaders can motivate others to stretch their limits, think outside the box, and pursue ambitious goals. These leaders willing to take risks can inspire team confidence, creativity, and boldness.

Failure can be a valuable learning opportunity that can lead to valuable insights, lessons learned, and personal or professional development. Of course, embracing risk is not about recklessness or blind ambition; Visionary leaders meticulously evaluate potential downsides and consequences, mitigating risks through strategic planning and calculated decision-making. They conduct thorough risk assessments, considering market demand, competitive landscape, resource requirements, and potential obstacles.

Risk-taking requires resilience and tenacity, as it often involves facing uncertainty, adversity, and setbacks along the way. Visionary leaders develop contingency plans and alternative strategies to lessen the impact of potential risks. They anticipate potential challenges and setbacks and prepare backup plans to address unexpected obstacles or changes in circumstances. Visionary leaders who take risks demonstrate courage, determination, and perseverance in facing challenges, inspiring others to do the same.

True Visionary leaders lead by example, demonstrating a willingness to take these risks and embrace uncertainty. They show courage, resilience, and tenacity in facing challenges, inspiring their teams to push boundaries and pursue ambitious goals. When risks pay off and lead to success, Visionary leaders celebrate achievements and recognize the contributions of their teams. They reinforce a culture of innovation and risk-taking by acknowledging and rewarding bold initiatives that drive positive outcomes.

Risk Is Inspirational

Communicating the value of risk to their teams is crucial for Visionary leaders to build a culture of innovation, empowerment, and continuous improvement. They use direct, to-the-point, inspirational methods to create optimism and faith in their teams' hearts and minds.

How do they do this effectively? By following these steps:

Articulate the Vision | Visionary leaders start by articulating a compelling vision highlighting the importance of innovation, growth, and adaptability. They explain how taking calculated risks aligns with the company's long-term goals and strategic objectives.

Provide Context | Visionary leaders explain why risk-taking is necessary by discussing market trends, competitive dynamics, and industry challenges. They help their teams understand the rationale behind risky decisions and how they contribute to the company's long-term success.

Share Success Stories | Visionary leaders share success stories and case studies demonstrating positive outcomes of risk-taking. They highlight examples of innovative projects or initiatives that have led to breakthroughs, competitive advantages, or new opportunities for the company.

Encourage Open Dialogue | Visionary leaders encourage open dialogue and discussion about risk within their teams. They create a safe environment where employees feel comfortable sharing their ideas, concerns, and perspectives on risk-taking.

Celebrate Failure as Learning | Visionary leaders reframe failure as a valuable learning opportunity rather than a negative outcome. They celebrate instances where employees take risks, regardless of the outcome, and encourage them to reflect on what they have learned from the experience.

Provide Support and Resources | Visionary leaders provide employees with the necessary support and resources to take risks responsibly. They allocate budget, time, and manpower for innovation projects, provide access to training and development opportunities, and offer mentorship and guidance.

Lead by Example | Visionary leaders lead by example, demonstrating their willingness to take risks and embrace uncertainty. They share their own experiences of risk-taking, including both successes and failures, and show vulnerability in acknowledging their own mistakes.

Set Clear Expectations | Visionary leaders set clear expectations for risk-taking within their teams, including guidelines, boundaries, and criteria for decision-making. They communicate the importance of balancing innovation with accountability and responsibility.

Recognize and Reward Risk-Taking | Visionary leaders recognize and reward employees who take risks and demonstrate creativity, initiative, and resilience. They publicly acknowledge and celebrate individuals or teams contributing to innovative solutions or successful outcomes through risk-taking.

Seek Feedback and Continuous Improvement | Visionary leaders seek feedback from their teams on how risk-taking is perceived and how it can be further encouraged and supported. They are open to suggestions for improvement and continuously refine their communication strategies to effectively convey the value of risk to their teams.

As we'll see in the example below, successful Visionary leaders use these techniques and others to motivate and inspire their teams and brands to generational greatness.

Risk Is Aspirational

Visionary leaders who take risks possess unique traits that enable them to navigate uncertainty, inspire innovation, and drive success. Visionaries are a rare breed, but they have shared traits that are common factors in achieving their success. Here are some key traits of Visionary leaders who are willing to take risks:

Courage | Visionary leaders exhibit courage in the face of uncertainty and adversity. They are willing to step outside their comfort zones, challenge the status quo, and pursue bold initiatives others may perceive as risky.

Strategic Vision | Visionary leaders clearly envision the future and understand how their actions fit into the bigger picture. They can identify opportunities for growth and innovation, even in the face of uncertainty, and develop strategic plans to capitalize on them.

Innovative Thinking | Visionary leaders are creative and innovative thinkers, unafraid to explore new ideas and approaches. They encourage creativity and experimentation within their organizations, fostering an environment where new ideas can flourish.

Resilience | Visionary leaders are resilient in the face of failure or setbacks. They view failure as a learning opportunity and can bounce back quickly from setbacks, using them as fuel for future success.

Confidence | Visionary leaders exude confidence and conviction in their decisions and actions. They trust their instincts and are not easily swayed by criticism or doubt. Their confidence inspires trust and loyalty in their teams, encouraging others to follow their lead.

Risk Management | While Visionary leaders are willing to take risks, they also understand the importance of strategic risk management. They carefully evaluate each opportunity's potential risks and rewards, develop contingency plans, and make informed decisions based on data and analysis.

Communication | Visionary leaders are skilled communicators who clearly articulate their team's vision, goals, and expectations. They inspire others with passion and enthusiasm, rallying support for their ideas and initiatives.

Empowerment | Visionary leaders empower their teams to take risks and make decisions independently. They create a culture of trust and empowerment, where employees feel encouraged to share their ideas, take initiative, and contribute to the organization's success.

Long-Term Thinking | Visionary leaders have a long-term orientation and are willing to invest in initiatives that may not pay off immediately but have the potential for significant long-term impact. They understand that taking risks is often necessary for meaningful progress and sustainable success.

Why Risk-Taking Matters

By leveraging the above practices and traits, Visionary leaders can navigate uncertainty, inspire creativity, and drive positive organizational change. Remember, a leader's legacy is not defined by the risks they avoided but by the bold chances they took, the uncharted waters they navigated, and the transformative impact they created for themselves and the brand they lead.

Risk-taking is integral to the success of Visionary leaders because it enables them to innovate, adapt, differentiate, inspire, and seize opportunities in pursuit of their vision. While not all risks will lead to success, embracing risk-taking as part of a strategic approach can drive growth, innovation, and sustainable success in the long run. Visionary leaders can drive innovation, growth, and sustainable brand success by embracing calculated risk-taking.

Attempt. Fail. Learn.

The Visionary | AMELIA EARHART

Never interrupt someone doing what you said couldn't be done.
– Amelia Earhart

Amelia Earhart (1897–1937) was an American aviation pioneer and one of the most iconic figures in aviation history. Her life was marked by groundbreaking achievements, courageous feats, and a relentless spirit of adventure. In other words, she is a perfect example of how risk can be anticipated, met, and conquered.

Amelia Mary Earhart was born on July 24, 1897, in Atchison, Kansas, USA. She spent her childhood exploring the outdoors and was fascinated with flying machines. After attending Hyde Park High School in Chicago, Illinois, Earhart enrolled at Ogontz School in Pennsylvania and later attended Columbia University but did not complete her degree.

Earhart's interest in aviation started in December 1920 when she attended an aerial exhibition in California. She took her first flying lesson in January 1921 and was determined to pursue an aviation career. In 1922, Earhart set her first aviation record by becoming the first woman to fly solo above 14,000 feet. In 1928, she gained international fame as the first woman to fly across the Atlantic Ocean, albeit as a passenger. This flight earned her widespread acclaim and propelled her to icon status. In 1932, Earhart achieved another milestone by becoming the first woman to fly solo nonstop across the Atlantic, flying from Newfoundland to Ireland in approximately 15 hours.

Over the years, Earhart set multiple aviation records for female pilots, including speed and altitude records. She was a passionate advocate for gender equality in aviation and worked to promote opportunities for women in the field. She co-founded The Ninety-Nines, an organization for female pilots, and served as its first president. She also used her fame to inspire young women to pursue careers in aviation and other male-dominated fields. She believed that women could achieve anything they set their minds to.

On July 2, 1937, Earhart and navigator Fred Noonan disappeared during an attempt to circle the globe in a Lockheed Model 10 Electra aircraft. Despite an extensive search effort, their remains and the wreckage of their plane were never found. Earhart's disappearance remains one of the greatest mysteries in aviation history, and numerous theories have been proposed to explain what happened to her. Despite her tragic end, Earhart's legacy inspires generations of aviators and adventurers.

THE RISK | 156

Earhart received numerous awards and honors throughout her life, including the United States Distinguished Flying Cross, which she received posthumously in 1939. Her legacy lives on through her contributions to aviation and her role as a symbol of courage, determination, and perseverance in the face of adversity.

In short, Amelia Earhart is widely considered a Visionary leader for her aviation successes and trailblazing spirit. Several characteristics contribute to Earhart's status as a Visionary:

Fearlessness | In her aviation career, Earhart faced numerous challenges and risks, including mechanical failures, unpredictable weather, and long and arduous flights. Her fearlessness in the face of these challenges reflected her pioneering spirit.

Breaking Gender Barriers | Earhart defied societal norms and gender stereotypes by embracing this risk and pursuing a career in aviation at a time when it was predominantly a male-dominated field. Her determination to succeed in a male-dominated industry made her a trailblazer for women's rights and paved the way for future generations of female aviators. As a vocal advocate for gender equality, her advocacy work helped create opportunities for women to pursue careers in aviation and encouraged them to break free from traditional gender roles.

Adventure and Exploration | Earhart's adventurous spirit and love of exploration captured the imagination of people around the world. Her daring flights and ambitious goals inspired countless individuals to pursue their dreams, explore new frontiers, and embrace a spirit of adventure.

Inspiring Generations | Even decades after her disappearance, Earhart's legacy inspires people of all ages to embrace risk, pursue their passions, and overcome obstacles. Her story serves as a reminder of the power of risk-taking, perseverance, resilience, and determination in adversity.

Independence | Earhart symbolized freedom, independence, and pursuing your dreams. Her life and achievements represented the triumph of the human spirit over adversity and inspired millions to believe in the power of their dreams and aspirations.

Determination | Earhart's courage and determination were evident in her decision to pursue a career in aviation during a time when flying was considered risky and daring. Her determination to overcome societal expectations and challenges demonstrated her Visionary spirit.

Vision | Earhart's vision for aviation's future extended beyond her achievements. She believed in aviation's potential to connect people and cultures and foresaw its role in shaping a more interconnected world.

Global Perspective | Earhart's flights took her to various parts of the world, and she developed a global perspective on aviation and its potential to bring people together. Her vision extended beyond national borders, emphasizing the role of aviation in advancing international understanding.

Inspirational Legacy | Amelia Earhart's legacy inspires individuals, especially women, to pursue careers in aviation and other male-dominated fields. Her achievements and the challenges she overcame contribute to her status as a Visionary and a role model.

Amelia Earhart's Visionary characteristics include her **courage, determination, advocacy for gender equality, vision for the future of her field, commitment to education, global perspective**, and perhaps most of all, her **fearlessness in taking calculated risks**. She challenged the status quo, pushed the boundaries of what was possible, and inspired generations to reach for the skies, literally and symbolically. Her groundbreaking achievements in aviation paved the way for future generations of pilots, and her legacy continues to inspire people worldwide to pursue their dreams, no matter the obstacles they may face.

ACCOMPLISHMENTS

First Female Aviator to Fly Solo Across the Atlantic | In 1932, Earhart became the first woman to fly solo nonstop across the Atlantic Ocean, setting a record by completing the flight in approximately 15 hours. This achievement marked a significant milestone in aviation history and solidified her status as a trailblazer for female pilots.

Aviation Records | Earhart set several aviation records for women and men. She became the first person to fly solo from Hawaii to the U.S. mainland and set the women's world altitude record by reaching an altitude of 14,000 feet in 1922.

Co-founder of The Ninety-Nines | In 1929, Earhart co-founded The Ninety-Nines, an organization for female pilots to provide mutual support and advance women's participation in aviation. The organization continues to promote women in aviation and aerospace today.

Transatlantic Passenger Flights | Earhart made history as the first woman to fly across the Atlantic Ocean as a passenger. In 1928, she flew as part of a transatlantic flight crew, becoming the first woman to make the journey by air.

Promoting Women's Rights and Aviation | Earhart used her fame to advocate for women's rights, particularly in aviation. She encouraged women to pursue careers in aviation and challenged gender stereotypes, inspiring generations of female pilots and adventurers.

The Visionary | FRANK LLOYD WRIGHT

There is nothing more uncommon than common sense.
– Frank Lloyd Wright

Frank Lloyd Wright (1867–1959) was an American architect, interior designer, writer, and educator, widely considered one of the greatest architects of the 20th century. His risk-taking, pioneering approach to architecture, characterized by organic integration with the natural environment and innovative use of materials, revolutionized the field and left a lasting impact on modern architecture.

Frank Lloyd Wright was born on June 8, 1867, in Richland Center, Wisconsin, USA. He grew up in a family of Welsh descent and was influenced by the simple, geometric forms of the Midwestern landscape.

Wright's interest in architecture was inspired at an early age. At 18, he began working as an apprentice to architect Joseph Lyman Silsbee in Chicago. He later worked for the firm of Adler & Sullivan, where he collaborated with renowned architect Louis Sullivan.

Wright's architectural style, known as "organic architecture," was characterized by harmony with nature, open floor plans, and innovative use of steel, concrete, and glass materials. He rejected the traditional European architectural styles of his time and sought to create uniquely American buildings that reflected the democratic ideals and natural beauty of the United States.

Wright's career spanned over seven decades and produced over 500 completed structures, including private residences, public buildings, and commercial projects. His most iconic works include the Robie House in Chicago, Fallingwater in Pennsylvania, Taliesin in Wisconsin, and the Guggenheim Museum in New York City. His innovative designs and philosophies had a deep influence on modern architecture and design, inspiring generations of architects around the world. Wright's emphasis on organic forms, integration with the natural environment, and use of new materials laid the foundation for many architectural movements, including the Prairie School, the International Style, and the organic architecture movement.

Frank Lloyd Wright was a risk-taking Visionary in numerous ways, contributing to his profound impact on architecture and design. Wright was known for challenging traditional architectural conventions and pushing the boundaries of what was considered possible in architecture. He rejected his contemporaries' ornate, historical styles and instead embraced a modern, forward-thinking approach to design. Wright's designs were characterized by innovative concepts ahead of his time. He experimented with open floor plans, horizontal lines, and seamless integration with the natural environment, defying conventional architectural norms and creating a new aesthetic language. Needless to say, this forward-thinking approach to design represented a significant risk to a working architect; his out-of-the-box designs had the potential to ostracize him from potential customers. Ultimately, Wright's risks paid off, and his legacy continues to this day.

Wright was fearless in experimenting with new materials and construction techniques in his projects. He pioneered using reinforced concrete, steel, and glass in architectural design, creating innovative and structurally sound structures. Wright's philosophy of organic architecture emphasized harmony with the natural environment and was a bold departure from conventional architectural practices. He sought to blur the boundaries between indoor and outdoor spaces, creating environments connected to their surroundings.

Throughout his career, Wright engaged in various entrepreneurial ventures that were considered risky at the time. He established his architectural practice, which allowed him greater creative freedom but also subjected him to financial uncertainty. Wright also ventured into speculative real estate development, designing and building entire communities based on his architectural principles. While some of these projects faced challenges, they demonstrated his willingness to take risks in pursuit of his vision.

Wright's risk-taking and Visionary approach to architecture has had a lasting impact. His ideas and designs inspired subsequent generations of architects and designers, shaping the trajectory of modern architecture and design. Some of his most notable strides in the field of architecture include:

Modern Design Principles | Wright's designs were characterized by innovative principles, including open floor plans, horizontal lines, and natural materials. His forward-thinking approach challenged traditional architectural norms and set new standards for modern design.

Unity of Form and Function | Wright's work exemplified that form should follow function. He believed buildings should be aesthetically pleasing and efficiently fulfill their intended purpose. This philosophy influenced the Modernist movement in architecture.

Architectural Innovations | Wright was known for introducing innovative architectural elements, such as the cantilevered balcony and the open-plan office. His designs often incorporated cutting-edge technologies and materials of his time.

Holistic Approach | Wright took a holistic approach to architecture, considering the entire building environment, including the landscape, climate, and occupants' lifestyles. His designs intended to create a harmonious relationship between the built environment and its surroundings.

Prairie School Movement | As a key figure in the Prairie School architectural movement, Wright rejected the ornate styles of the time and embraced a more functional and aesthetically unified approach. His Prairie-style homes featured open interiors, flat or hipped roofs with broad overhanging eaves, and horizontal lines.

Architectural Diversity | Throughout his career, Wright employed a broad architectural language, adapting his style to suit various project requirements. His work showcased versatility and adaptability from Prairie-style homes to the iconic Fallingwater residence and the Guggenheim Museum.

Personal and Artistic Expression | Wright viewed architecture as a form of personal and artistic expression. He believed in creating unique and individualized designs tailored to the clients' needs and preferences, in contrast to the mass-produced architecture of his time.

Masterful Use of Space and Light | Wright's designs demonstrated a masterful use of space and light. He manipulated spatial arrangements and incorporated innovative lighting techniques to create dynamic and aesthetically pleasing interiors.

Educational Advocacy | Wright was passionate about educating aspiring architects. He founded the Taliesin Fellowship, an architectural apprenticeship program, to mentor and train the next generation of architects. This commitment to education contributed to the dissemination of his architectural principles.

Wright's career spanned several decades, and his influence still persists. His ideas and designs inspire architects and shape contemporary discussions about sustainable and thoughtful design. Despite facing numerous personal and professional challenges throughout his life, Wright remained dedicated to his craft and continued to produce groundbreaking architectural works until his death. During his life he received numerous awards and honors, including the AIA Gold Medal and the Royal Gold Medal for Architecture, and his works have been designated as UNESCO World Heritage Sites.

Frank Lloyd Wright's life and work exemplify creativity, innovation, and a deep connection to the natural world. His Visionary approach to architecture inspires architects, designers, and enthusiasts worldwide, leaving an indelible mark on the built environment and the cultural landscape of the 20th century.

Wright's Visionary characteristics include his **innovative design principles**, **leadership in his industry**, **emphasis on the unity of form and function**, **holistic approach**, **personal and artistic expression**, **educational advocacy**, and **risk-taking approach to his discipline**. His impact on the architectural landscape and his enduring influence mark him as a Visionary figure in the history of architecture.

ACCOMPLISHMENTS

Fallingwater | Completed in 1939, Fallingwater is one of Wright's most iconic works. This house is located in Pennsylvania and is renowned for integrating with the natural environment, as it was built over a waterfall. Fallingwater exemplifies Wright's organic architecture philosophy, harmonizing the man-made structure with the surrounding landscape.

Innovations in Design | Wright pioneered various architectural innovations, including cantilevered balconies and integrated natural elements. He also developed the "open plan," emphasizing spaciousness and flow between interior spaces.

Unity Temple | Located in Oak Park, Illinois, Unity Temple is a prominent example of Wright's early work in modern architecture. Completed in 1908, it is considered one of the first modern buildings in the world. The temple's innovative use of reinforced concrete and geometric forms reflects Wright's architectural vision.

Prairie Style Architecture | Wright developed the Prairie style of architecture, characterized by horizontal lines, flat or hipped roofs with broad overhanging eaves, and integration with the natural surroundings. This style became synonymous with his early work and represented a departure from the dominant architectural styles of his time.

Taliesin and Taliesin West | Wright designed and built his home, Taliesin, in Spring Green, Wisconsin. He continually expanded and modified the residence throughout his life. Later, he established Taliesin West in Arizona as his winter home, studio, and architectural school. Both sites preserve Wright's legacy as architectural landmarks and educational institutions.

Usonian Houses | Wright developed the concept of Usonian houses to create affordable and functional homes for the American middle class. These houses often featured open floor plans, flat roofs, and innovative use of materials. Wright designed numerous Usonian homes, showcasing his vision for democratic and accessible architecture.

Guggenheim Museum | One of Wright's most famous designs, the Solomon R. Guggenheim Museum in New York City was completed in 1959. Its innovative spiral structure and open atrium challenged traditional museum design and provided a new way for visitors to experience art exhibitions.

Theoretical Contributions | Wright's writings and lectures on architecture, aesthetics, and society significantly influenced architectural theory and practice. His ideas on organic architecture, where buildings are in harmony with the natural environment and the needs of the inhabitants, continue to inspire architects and designers worldwide.

Chapter 11 | The FAILURES & SUCCESSES

My great concern is not whether you have failed,
but whether you are content with your failure.
– Abraham Lincoln

Visionary leaders recognize that failure is an inevitable part of the journey toward success. They leverage failures as valuable learning experiences and opportunities for growth, learning, and continuous innovation. These leaders embrace failure by fostering a culture that views failure as a natural part of the road toward success.

Leaning into failure is how one builds a true growth mindset, viewing failures as opportunities for learning and improvement rather than setbacks. They believe failure does not reflect a shortcoming in their abilities but rather a natural step toward success. When faced with failure, Visionary leaders take the time to analyze what went wrong and extract valuable lessons from the experience. They identify causes, patterns, and areas for improvement, enabling them to make better-informed decisions in the future. They recognize that innovation often requires taking risks and supports calculated experimentation, even if it fails.

Failure Is A Process

Visionary leaders create a culture that encourages innovation and risk-taking by embracing failure as an essential part of the creative process. They allow their teams to experiment, knowing that failure is often a necessary precursor to innovation and breakthroughs. They lead by example, demonstrating perseverance in adversity and inspiring others to do the same. A common understanding with Visionary leaders is that failure is not a dead end but rather an opportunity to iterate and adapt.

They create an environment where employees feel safe to experiment, knowing failure is not stigmatized but seen as an integral path to success. They create environments where failure is embraced and ultimately celebrated as instrumental in achieving their goals and realizing their vision. Visionary leaders support and encourage their teams after failure, offering guidance, feedback, and tools to help them rebound and move forward. They demonstrate empathy and understanding, recognizing that failure can be a challenging experience, and reward initiative and resilience in the face of failure. They recognize and celebrate individuals and teams who courageously take risks and bounce back from setbacks.

By promoting a growth mindset within their organizations, Visionary leaders emphasize the importance of learning from failure and seeing setbacks as opportunities for growth. They encourage their teams to adopt a positive attitude towards failure, viewing it as a chance to develop new skills and insights. Visionary leaders facilitate reflection and learning following failure, encouraging their teams to analyze what went wrong, what can be learned from the experience, and how to improve. They provide space for open and honest conversations about failure, fostering a culture of continuous improvement.

Finally, in addition to inviting the lessons from failure, Visionary leaders celebrate progress and successes, no matter how small, along the journey toward their ultimate vision. They recognize that success is often the result of many failures and setbacks overcome, and they acknowledge and appreciate their teams' efforts along the way.

Failure Is Normal

Everyone will encounter failure at some point, especially those who attempt truly fearless goals. Visionary leaders lead by example, openly acknowledging their failures and setbacks. By sharing their experiences of failure and demonstrating resilience in the face of adversity, they set a tone that failure is acceptable and can be overcome. They will use feedback from failures to refine their strategies, adjust their approach, and pivot, if necessary, but not from their ultimate vision. They will move closer to their goals with each failure.

Of course, while Visionary leaders encourage risk-taking, they also promote accountability and responsibility. They hold themselves and their teams accountable for their actions and decisions, fostering a culture of ownership and continuous improvement. Visionary leaders cultivate resilience and tenacity in themselves and their teams, enabling them to bounce back from failure more decisive and determined.

In the face of setbacks and failures, Visionary leaders focus on the big picture and the ultimate vision they are working towards. They understand that failure is a temporary obstacle and remain committed to their long-term goals, adjusting their course as needed while staying true to their vision. They encourage a culture of reflection and continuous improvement, extracting insights from past experiences to inform future decisions.

Visionary leaders inspire their teams through failures by reframing setbacks as opportunities for growth, learning, and success. This can be accomplished through practices such as:

Normalizing Failure | Visionary leaders normalize failure by fostering a culture in which mistakes are seen as a natural part of the learning process. They emphasize that failure is not a reflection of incompetence but rather an inevitable aspect of taking risks and pursuing ambitious goals.

Sharing Personal Experiences | Visionary leaders share their own experiences of failure and resilience, demonstrating that setbacks are temporary and can be overcome with perseverance and determination. By showing vulnerability and authenticity, they inspire empathy and solidarity among team members.

Iterative Learning | Visionary leaders emphasize the learning opportunity inherent in failure. They encourage their teams to reflect on what went wrong, what could have been done differently, and what valuable lessons can be gleaned from the experience.

Progressive Failure | Visionary leaders reframe failure as progress toward success. They remind their teams that every setback brings them one step closer to their goals by providing valuable insights, revealing areas for improvement, and strengthening their resilience.

Futurecasting | Instead of dwelling on failure, Visionary leaders focus on identifying progressive solutions and taking decisive action to move forward. They empower their teams to brainstorm innovative ideas, pivot when necessary, and chart a new course toward success.

Mentorship | Visionary leaders support and encourage their teams during challenging times. They offer reassurance, mentorship, and resources to help team members rebound from failure and regain their confidence.

Celebration | Visionary leaders celebrate progress and small wins along the way, recognizing the effort and resilience demonstrated by their teams. They reinforce the idea that success is not defined by avoiding failure but by how one responds to it and continues to persevere.

Sustained Momentum | Visionaries don't allow failure (or success) to interrupt their progress; instead, they stay focused on the long-term vision and continue to drive progress toward their goals. They adapt to changing circumstances, seize new opportunities, and inspire others to remain committed to the journey.

By implementing these strategies, a Visionary leader can galvanize their team to drive continual success in creating products that meet customer needs, exceed expectations, and make a meaningful impact in the marketplace. Inspiring their teams through failures, Visionary leaders create a culture of resilience, innovation, and continuous improvement, enabling their organizations to overcome challenges and achieve greater success in the long run.

Failure to Success

Success consists of going from failure to failure without loss of enthusiasm.
– Winston Churchill

Visionary leaders stand apart through their distinctive ability to transform failure into success, guiding their teams through adversity to achievement. Their resilience serves as a cornerstone, allowing them to rebound from setbacks and ingeniously use failure as a catalyst for growth. In the face of an ever-changing landscape, these leaders display remarkable adaptability, constantly fine-tuning their strategies to navigate unforeseen obstacles.

Transparency and open communication are their weapons of choice when confronting challenges, fostering a culture of trust and collective problem-solving. Their high emotional intelligence enables them to empathize with their team, turning the ashes of failure into the phoenix of success. By intimately understanding each team member's unique strengths and needs, these leaders provide tailored support and encouragement, maintaining high morale even in the darkest hours. At the core of their leadership philosophy lies a growth mindset, embracing failure as an integral part of the learning journey. This perspective, coupled with their unwavering commitment to the vision, instills confidence and trust throughout the organization. Visionary leaders don't just manage teams; they inspire, adapt, and persevere, turning potential disasters into stepping stones for unprecedented success.

These traits empower Visionary leaders to navigate adversity, foster resilience, and ultimately lead their teams to eventual success through inevitable failures. Visionary leaders move from failure to success by adopting a relentless mindset, embracing failure as a learning opportunity, and leveraging setbacks to fuel growth and innovation. Here are the practices by which they accomplish this transition from failure to success:

Acknowledge Failure | Visionary leaders acknowledge failure openly and honestly, without placing blame or making excuses. They take ownership of the situation and recognize that failure is a natural part of the journey towards success.

Extract Lessons | Instead of dwelling on failure, Visionary leaders focus on extracting valuable lessons from the experience. They reflect on what went wrong, why it happened, and what could be done differently in the future to avoid similar mistakes.

Maintain Perspective | Visionary leaders maintain a long-term perspective, understanding that failure is often a temporary setback on the path to success. They remind themselves and their teams that setbacks are growth opportunities and that success is achieved through perseverance and resilience.

Commit to the Vision | Visionary leaders remain steadfastly committed to their vision and goals despite setbacks and challenges. They remind themselves and their teams of the larger purpose behind their work, inspiring them to stay focused and determined to pursue their objectives.

Adapt and Pivot | Visionary leaders are agile and adaptive in response to failure, willing to pivot and change course as needed. They use failure as an opportunity to reassess their strategies, adjust their approach, and explore new opportunities for innovation and growth.

Inspire Resilience | Visionary leaders inspire resilience and perseverance in their teams, leading by demonstrating resilience in the face of adversity.

Encourage Risk-Taking | Visionary leaders encourage risk-taking and experimentation within their teams, recognizing that innovation often involves taking calculated risks. They create a culture where failure is not punished but celebrated as a sign of creativity and initiative.

Learn, Iterate, and Improve | Visionary leaders embrace a continuous improvement mindset, using failure as a catalyst for learning, iteration, and improvement. They apply the lessons from failure to refine their strategies, innovate their products, and drive future success.

Why Failure Matters

By always being committed to their vision, embracing failure as a natural part of the journey, and using these as opportunities for growth and learning, Visionary leaders ultimately move from failure to success, achieving their goals and realizing their vision for the future. Through it all, Visionary leaders steadfastly focus on the organization's vision and long-term goals. They remind their teams that failure is temporary and that setbacks are opportunities for greater success in pursuing the shared vision.

Fail. Learn. Succeed.

The Visionary | THOMAS EDISON

Genius is one percent inspiration and ninety-nine percent perspiration.
– Thomas Edison

One of history's most inexhaustible inventors, Thomas Edison (February 11, 1847 – October 18, 1931), had a remarkable mind that contributed to groundbreaking inventions. His creative process and approach to generating ideas for inventions were multifaceted and involved a combination of innovative thinking, extensive experimentation, and relentless determination.

How did Edison so skillfully move from failure to failure to eventual and unparalleled success? His keen observational ability, among other things, allowed him to identify problems and inefficiencies in existing systems. He approached invention as a means of solving practical problems to improve people's lives.

Edison embraced an iterative approach to innovation. He understood that success often came through repeated experimentation and refinement of his ideas. His famous quote reflects this mindset: "I have not failed. I've just found 10,000 ways that won't work." Rather than focusing solely on hypothetical concepts, Edison was interested in applying scientific knowledge to real-world problems; that is, the practical needs of the world often drove his inventions. Edison could identify problems and create solutions proactively. Whether improving existing technologies or creating new ones, he approached barriers with a problem-solving mindset that was the cornerstone of his success as an inventor.

As an entrepreneur, Edison conceived ideas and worked tirelessly to bring them to market. His inventions were not just concepts but products with practical applications. To realize his ideas, Edison recognized the value of collaboration and teamwork. To further his skill in realizing his ideas, he established the world's first industrial research laboratory in Menlo Park, New Jersey, bringing together a team of scientists, engineers, and inventors to work collectively on projects. His ability to lead and inspire this team of engineers and inventors was crucial to the success of his many projects. This team mastermind concept would be integral to Edison's success and would contribute to future similar concepts that have since developed some of the world's greatest inventions.

Edison had a wide range of interests and expertise. His inventions spanned various fields, from the phonograph to the electric light bulb to the motion picture camera, showcasing his ability to apply knowledge from diverse markets. Known for his relentless experimentation, he systematically tested thousands of variations to find the most effective solutions. He approached problems by breaking them down into manageable components.

This methodical problem-solving approach allowed him to address challenges methodically and incrementally.

Thomas Edison was not only an inventor but also a skilled promoter. He engaged with the public, showcasing his inventions through public demonstrations and exhibitions. His ability to communicate the potential of his innovations contributed to their widespread acceptance and adoption. Edison maintained an optimistic outlook and a high level of perseverance. Despite facing numerous setbacks and failures, he viewed challenges as opportunities to learn and refine his ideas.

Edison recognized the importance of protecting his intellectual property. He secured numerous patents for his inventions, providing legal safeguards for his innovations. Edison held over 1,000 patents for his inventions, showcasing his idea-generator mindset and foundational passion for improving the world. His ability to consistently generate new ideas and bring them to fruition demonstrated a Visionary approach to problem-solving and technology.

Edison faced many failures and setbacks throughout his career, particularly in his journey to invent the electric light bulb. His experiments in pursuit of this goal involved testing thousands of different filament materials, trying various bulb designs, and developing supporting infrastructure for electric lighting systems. Along the way, Edison encountered innumerable barriers and disappointments, all easily visible in the abandoned prototypes or designs. However, Edison's persistence eventually paid off, and in 1879, he successfully developed a practical incandescent light bulb with a carbonized bamboo filament that could provide long-lasting illumination. If Edison had given up this goal after encountering failure, the world would be a darker place for it!

Edison was aware of market needs and demands, creating inventions with widespread use and appeal, ensuring their commercial success. He was quick to embrace new and emerging technologies, was not bound by traditional methods, and utilized cutting-edge advancements to improve his inventions. Edison focused on creating inventions that had broad applications and could be commercialized. This uncompromising process distinguishes him as a Visionary who understood the importance of turning ideas into tangible products that could benefit the world. Edison invented products and had a vision for how they could be integrated into the market and responded with an adaptable and agile mindset when an invention proved a failure, either mechanically or commercially.

Thomas Edison's mind was characterized by a unique combination of creativity, practicality, and a relentless pursuit of innovation. His approach to invention has left a lasting mark on the technology field and inspires aspiring inventors and innovators. Edison's inventions, such as the phonograph and the electric light bulb, had a profound and lasting impact on society. He played a key role in establishing the electric power industry, demonstrating his ability to envision the broader global impact of his inventions. His Visionary contributions laid the foundation for the modern technological era, influencing subsequent generations of inventors and entrepreneurs.

Thomas Edison's Visionary characteristics include **an inventive mindset, creative application of ideas, relentless persistence, team inspiration and collaboration, future vision, diversification of interests, public engagement, entrepreneurial spirit,** and **a bottomless willingness to learn from failure.** These characteristics and his many significant accomplishments earned Thomas Edison the nickname "The Wizard of Menlo Park." His innovations transformed industries and shaped the modern world, laying the groundwork for many technologies we use today.

ACCOMPLISHMENTS

Electric Light Bulb | Edison is widely credited with inventing the modern-day incandescent light bulb. Although he did not invent the first light bulb, his design was the first to be commercially viable, making electric lighting accessible to the public.

Phonograph | Edison invented the phonograph, which recorded and reproduced sound. It began the modern music and entertainment industry, allowing audio recordings to be conserved and shared.

Motion Pictures | Edison contributed significantly to the development of motion pictures. He invented the kinetoscope, a device for viewing moving images, and established the first motion picture production studio. His innovations laid the foundation for the film industry.

Electric Power Distribution System | Edison developed a practical electric power distribution system, including power plants, transformers, and distribution lines. His system helped establish the framework for modern electrical grids, enabling the widespread adoption of electric power for homes and businesses.

Storage Batteries | Edison improved existing storage battery technology, making batteries more practical and reliable. His advancements in battery technology have applications in various industries, including transportation and telecommunications.

Dictating Machine | Edison invented the phonographic cylinder-based dictating machine, which allowed individuals to record spoken words and play them back. This device was widely used in business and administrative settings.

Improvements to the Telegraph | Edison made several improvements to the telegraph, including the invention of a duplex telegraph system, which allowed two messages to be sent simultaneously on a single wire. He also developed a quadruplex telegraph system, further increasing the efficiency of telegraph communication.

Carbon Microphone | Edison invented the carbon microphone, a crucial component in early telephones. His microphone design significantly improved the clarity and quality of voice communication over telephone lines.

Research and Development Lab | Edison established the world's first industrial research and development laboratory in Menlo Park, New Jersey. This laboratory became a model for future research facilities and significantly influenced Edison's inventive successes.

Chapter 12 | The TORCH

A genuine leader is not a searcher for
consensus but a molder of consensus.
– Dr. Martin Luther King Jr.

The mantle of leadership carries with it a dual responsibility: to innovate boldly and to honor the legacy of those who came before. As new leaders step into their roles, they are tasked with more than just maintaining the status quo. Their mission is to push the boundaries of possibility, to challenge conventional wisdom, and to forge new paths in their industries and communities. This forward-thinking approach, however, must be balanced with a deep respect for the foundations laid by their predecessors. By building upon the achievements and lessons of the past, leaders can create a bridge between established wisdom and cutting-edge innovation. In doing so, they ensure that the contributions of previous generations continue to influence and shape our collective future.

This delicate balance of honoring history while driving progress is what distinguishes truly Visionary leaders. They understand that their role is not just to lead in the present, but to create a legacy that will inspire and guide future generations. By embracing this philosophy, leaders can elevate their organizations, their industries, and indeed, our shared experience to new levels, creating a future that is both rooted in respected traditions and open to transformative possibilities. This chapter is specifically aimed at those taking up a new leadership position to better prepare them to carry the torch as a true Visionary.

Accepting the Torch

Carrying the torch that was lit and carried by previous generations of Visionary leaders requires tact, humility, and a deep respect for the legacy and contributions of one's forebears. This challenge is most prominent when one takes on a new position in an organization, and must be handled with great care by any leader.

A new leader can gracefully transition into their role by first expressing gratitude and appreciation for the foundation laid by their predecessor. Acknowledging a previous leader's achievements, values, and vision sets a positive tone for the transition and honors their legacy. The new leader must demonstrate a willingness to listen and learn from the experiences and insights of the outgoing leader, recognizing the value of their wisdom and perspective.

New leaders also must ensure that their own vision aligns with the organization's core values and mission. While bringing their unique perspective and ideas to the table, they should strive to uphold the principles and commitments established by their predecessors. Communicating continuity and evolution is essential in this process. By acknowledging past achievements while articulating their vision for the future, new leaders can inspire confidence and trust among stakeholders.

At the same time, a leader's job is not to merely imitate their predecessor or abandon their own vision in favor of continuing the old way; they need to authentically and transparently communicate their own vision and leadership style. By articulating their vision for the organization's future while also recognizing the importance of continuity, the new leader can inspire confidence and trust among team members. The new leader must foster open communication and collaboration, inviting feedback and input from team members as they navigate the transition together.

When new Visionary leaders step into roles previously held by other leaders, they face the delicate task of honoring the established legacy while injecting their innovative spirit into the organization. One method they can use to carry on the tradition of a previous Visionary leader is to study and deeply understand the legacy left behind. By immersing themselves in the organization's history, values, and past achievements, new leaders can gain valuable insights into the vision and strategies implemented by their predecessors.

The new leader should prioritize building relationships and trust with stakeholders at all levels of the organization. By demonstrating empathy, integrity, and a genuine commitment to the organization's mission, the new leader can earn the respect and support of their team and lay the foundation for a successful transition. Meanwhile, by seeking guidance and understanding from those who worked closely with the previous Visionary leader, new leaders can gain a deeper appreciation for the organization's culture and values. Throughout the process, humility and modesty are essential as the new leader recognizes that they stand on the shoulders of those who came before them.

Passing on the Torch

Carrying the torch is an important task, and like all such duties, it's not to be undertaken alone; empowering and inspiring the team to continue their organization's legacy of excellence is critical. New leaders should build a culture of advancement, proactive collaboration, and accountability, encouraging team members to contribute their ideas and talents toward achieving shared goals.

Of course, encouraging your team to embrace change and adaptation is also essential. While respecting the organization's traditions, new leaders should be open to new ideas, technologies, and market dynamics and be willing to pivot and adjust strategies to stay relevant and competitive. Leading by example and seeking stakeholder feedback and collaboration further solidifies the transition. By embodying the organization's culture and values while setting a clear vision and direction for the future, new leaders can honor the legacy of their predecessors while propelling the organization forward into a new era of growth and success.

Instilling confidence in a new team as a Visionary leader requires a multifaceted approach that combines clear communication, inspirational leadership, and supportive actions. The new leader must establish open communication channels, articulating the brand's vision, mission, and goals with clarity and enthusiasm. By providing a clear roadmap for the future, team members gain a sense of purpose and direction, instilling confidence in the leader's vision. The leader inspires trust and respect among team members through their unwavering commitment to the brand's values and principles, fostering a positive and supportive work environment.

Additionally, a new leader should prioritize providing support and resources to the team, ensuring they have the tools and training necessary to succeed in their roles. By offering mentorship, guidance, and encouragement, the leader empowers team members to overcome challenges and excel in their work, further boosting their confidence.

Furthermore, the leader should promote a culture of collaboration, encouraging open dialogue, mutual respect, and collective problem-solving. By creating a sense of community and shared purpose, team members feel valued and supported, reinforcing their confidence in the leader and their colleagues. Consistently celebrating successes and achievements as a team is essential for building trust and morale. Recognizing individual contributions and collective accomplishments fosters a sense of pride and accomplishment, reinforcing the team's belief in their ability to achieve great things together.

Finally, the new leader should emphasize a mindset of continuous improvement and learning, encouraging team members to embrace feedback, seek out new opportunities, and grow both personally and professionally. By promoting a culture of growth and development, the leader demonstrates their commitment to the team's success, further instilling confidence in their leadership.

Through clear communication, inspirational leadership, and supportive actions, a new leader can effectively instill confidence in their team, empowering them to achieve extraordinary results and drive the brand forward to success—that's how a Visionary leader ensures the torch is carried on through the next generation.

Keeping the Torch Lit

When a Visionary leader steps into a new role, they often face the challenge of maintaining the legacy and vision established by their predecessors while bringing their unique perspectives and ideas to the table. Taking up the mantle of leadership at a Visionary brand necessitates deploying some methods to carry on the tradition of a previous Visionary leader:

Study and Understand the Legacy | New Visionary leaders should take the time to study and understand the previous leader's legacy. They should familiarize themselves with the organization's history, values, culture, past successes, and the vision and strategies implemented by their predecessor.

Build Relationships and Seek Guidance | New Visionary leaders must build relationships with key stakeholders, including board members, senior executives, employees, and customers. They should seek guidance and insights from those who worked closely with the previous leader to better understand their vision and approach.

Align with Core Values and Mission | New Visionary

leaders should ensure that their values and vision align with the core values and mission of the organization established by their predecessors. They should uphold the organization's principles and commitments while bringing their unique perspective and ideas.

Communicate Continuity and Evolution | New Visionary leaders should emphasize continuity and evolution when communicating with stakeholders. They should acknowledge the previous leader's achievements and successes while articulating their vision for the future and how it builds upon the foundation laid by their predecessor.

Empower and Inspire the Team | New Visionary leaders should empower and inspire their team members to continue pursuing the organization's mission and vision. They should foster a culture of innovation, collaboration, and accountability, encouraging team members to contribute their ideas and talents toward achieving shared goals.

Embrace Change and Adaptation | While respecting the organization's traditions and legacy, new Visionary leaders should also be willing to embrace change and adaptation as needed. They should be open to new ideas, technologies, and market dynamics and willing to pivot and adjust strategies to stay relevant and competitive.

Build Trust | New Visionary leaders should lead by example, demonstrating the values, behaviors, and work ethic they expect from others. They should embody the organization's culture and values while also setting a clear vision and direction for the future.

Seek Feedback and Collaborate | Finally, new Visionary leaders should seek feedback and collaboration from stakeholders at all levels of the organization. They should be receptive to input and ideas from employees, customers, and other stakeholders, fostering a culture of transparency, inclusion, and continuous improvement.

By following these methods, Visionary leaders can honor the legacy of their predecessors while also bringing fresh perspectives and ideas to the organization, ensuring its continued growth, success, and relevance in the future.

Why Carrying the Torch Matters

In short, a Visionary leader is charged with embodying the values and principles of the organization and demonstrating their dedication to serving the best interests of the team and their company. By approaching the transition with grace, humility, and a commitment to building upon the legacy of their predecessor, the new leader can effectively take the torch and lead the organization into a new chapter of growth, innovation, and success.

Analyze. Embrace. Lead.

The Visionary | SATYA NADELLA

Every opportunity I got, I took it as a learning experience.
– Satya Nadella

Satya Narayana Nadella, born on August 19, 1967, is a Visionary leader and the current CEO of Microsoft Corporation. Nadella's life story is marked by his journey from humble beginnings to becoming one of the most influential technology leaders.

Nadella grew up in Hyderabad, India, where he developed a passion for technology from a young age. He attended Manipal Institute of Technology, earning a bachelor's degree in electrical engineering. He later moved to the United States to pursue further education, earning a master's degree in computer science from the University of Wisconsin–Milwaukee and an MBA from the University of Chicago Booth School of Business.

Nadella joined Microsoft in 1992, quickly rising through the ranks thanks to his technical acumen and leadership skills. Over the years, he held various roles within the company, including Senior Vice President of Research and Development for the Online Services Division and Server & Tools Division President. In 2014, Nadella was appointed as the CEO of Microsoft, succeeding Steve Ballmer.

As CEO, Nadella has led Microsoft through a period of transformation and innovation, steering the company towards a cloud-first, mobile-first strategy. Under his leadership, Microsoft has embraced cloud computing by introducing Azure, a leading cloud platform. It has shifted its focus towards subscription-based services such as Office 365 and Microsoft 365. Nadella has also overseen several strategic acquisitions, including the purchase of LinkedIn in 2016 and GitHub in 2018. He has also championed initiatives around artificial intelligence, mixed reality, and quantum computing, positioning Microsoft at the forefront of technological innovation.

Since becoming CEO of Microsoft in 2014, Nadella has led the company through significant transformation and innovation, positioning it as a leader in cloud computing, artificial intelligence, and other cutting-edge technologies. According to the company's new mission statement, Nadella's vision for Microsoft is centered around "empowering every person and every organization on the planet to achieve more." Under his leadership, Microsoft has embraced a cloud-first, mobile-first strategy, focusing on delivering innovative solutions and services to customers across various industries.

Beyond his strategic vision for the company, Nadella is known for his leadership philosophy, emphasizing empathy, humility, and a growth mindset. He has prioritized diversity and inclusion within Microsoft, leading efforts to promote gender and racial diversity in the company's workforce and culture. Nadella has become famous for his leadership philosophy, emphasizing empathy, a growth mindset, and a commitment to diversity and inclusion. He authored a book titled *Hit Refresh*, in which he shares his journey and vision for the future of technology.

When Satya Nadella took up the torch by assuming the CEO role at Microsoft in 2014, he inherited a company facing several significant challenges following Steve Ballmer's departure. One of the foremost challenges was navigating the rapidly evolving technology landscape. Microsoft, a stalwart in the industry, was grappling with shifts away from traditional revenue models such as Windows licensing, towards cloud computing, mobile devices, and subscription-based services. Nadella needed to steer Microsoft through this transition, ensuring the company remained competitive and relevant in changing market dynamics.

The cultural transformation was another major hurdle. Under Ballmer's leadership, Microsoft had developed a reputation for being a highly competitive and sometimes insular organization. Nadella recognized the need to foster a more inclusive, collaborative, and growth-oriented culture within the company. This required overcoming resistance to change and instilling a new mindset and values throughout the organization.

Also, Microsoft faced intense competition from industry giants like Amazon Web Services (AWS) and Google Cloud Platform in the cloud computing market. Nadella had to accelerate Microsoft's efforts in cloud computing, differentiate Azure from competitors, and expand the company's market share and revenue in this critical area. The same pressure was present when it came to Microsoft's mobile strategy. Under Ballmer's leadership, the company had struggled to gain traction in the mobile device market, particularly with its Windows Phone platform. Nadella needed to reassess Microsoft's approach to mobile and determine how to compete effectively in a market dominated by iOS and Android devices.

In response to these challenges, Nadella sought to reignite Microsoft's focus on innovation and productivity. This involved fostering a culture of innovation, accelerating the pace of product development, and delivering innovative solutions to meet customers' evolving needs.

Finally, Nadella had to balance the continued support and development of legacy products and services, such as Windows, Office, and on-premises server software, with investments in newer, more innovative technologies and services. This required strategic decision-making to ensure Microsoft remained competitive while continuing to meet the needs of its diverse customer base.

When Satya Nadella took the helm at Microsoft, he faced complex challenges requiring him to navigate industry shifts, drive cultural change, compete in new markets, accelerate innovation, and strike a balance between legacy and future-focused initiatives. In response, he transformed Microsoft's culture, strategy, and product focus to adapt to a rapidly changing tech landscape while maintaining the company's historic dominance. His leadership and strategic initiatives have been instrumental in overcoming these challenges and positioning Microsoft for continued success and growth in the years ahead. His ability to successfully navigate these challenges has been a key factor in Microsoft's resurgence under his leadership.

Overall, Satya Nadella's Visionary leadership has been instrumental in shaping Microsoft's trajectory and solidifying its position as one of the world's leading technology companies. His **strategic vision**, **innovative thinking**, and **commitment to empowering others** have earned him widespread recognition and admiration as a true Visionary leader in the technology industry and beyond.

ACCOMPLISHMENTS

Cloud Computing Leadership | Under Nadella's leadership, Microsoft has become a dominant force in cloud computing. He spearheaded the development and expansion of Microsoft Azure, the company's cloud platform, which has grown rapidly to become one of the leading cloud services globally, competing with industry giants like Amazon Web Services (AWS) and Google Cloud Platform.

Subscription-Based Services | Nadella has shifted Microsoft's focus towards subscription-based services such as Office 365 and Microsoft 365. These services offer customers access to a suite of productivity tools and applications on a subscription basis, providing a steady and recurring revenue stream for the company.

Strategic Acquisitions | Nadella has overseen several strategic acquisitions that have expanded Microsoft's portfolio and capabilities. Notable acquisitions include the purchase of LinkedIn in 2016 for $26.2 billion, which strengthened Microsoft's presence in the professional networking and social media space, and GitHub in 2018 for $7.5 billion, which bolstered Microsoft's position in software development and collaboration tools.

Focus on Artificial Intelligence | Nadella has strongly emphasized artificial intelligence (AI) and machine learning as key areas of investment for Microsoft. He has championed initiatives to integrate AI capabilities into Microsoft's products and services, enabling customers to leverage AI-driven insights and capabilities to drive innovation and productivity.

Cultural Transformation | Nadella has led a cultural transformation within Microsoft, fostering a more inclusive, collaborative, and growth-oriented culture. He has prioritized diversity and inclusion initiatives, launched programs to promote employee development and learning, and encouraged a growth mindset throughout the organization.

Financial Performance | Under Nadella's leadership, Microsoft's financial performance has reached new heights. The company's market capitalization has soared, making it one of the most valuable companies in the world. Nadella's strategic vision and execution have driven strong revenue growth and profitability for Microsoft, delivering value to shareholders and stakeholders.

Chapter 13 | THE SOUL

Don't gain the world and lose your soul; wisdom
is better than silver or gold.

– Bob Marley

A Visionary leader is more than just a figurehead; they are the living embodiment of their brand or company's essence. These leaders infuse every facet of their leadership with the organization's core values, vision, and mission, becoming inseparable from the brand itself.

Consider the legendary Henry Ford, whose personal narrative and Visionary qualities have become so intertwined with his namesake company that they are now virtually indistinguishable. Or for a more recent example, look no further than Elon Musk, whose persona has become inextricably linked with the brand identities of the companies he leads. This synergy between leader and brand places enormous pressure on these visionaries to uphold and protect their organization's integrity.

A Visionary leader understands the delicate art of cultivating this image, carefully nurturing and maintaining the organization's soul in a manner that aligns perfectly with their grand vision. They recognize that their personal and company brands are two sides of the same coin, reinforcing and elevating the other. In this way, Visionary leaders don't just guide their organizations; they become the living, breathing heart and soul of their brand's promise and potential.

Visionaries drive the organization's purpose, inspiring others with passion, commitment, and innovation. Their actions and decisions set the tone for the organization's culture, establishing norms of behavior, communication, and collaboration that reflect the brand's identity and ethos. They lead by example, demonstrating integrity, authenticity, and a strong work ethic, inspiring trust and respect among their followers.

The Soul Is Aspirational

Visionary leaders inspire and align the team's efforts toward common goals and aspirations by communicating a clear and compelling vision for the future. How that vision is interpreted and applied—the company's soul—ultimately relies upon the behavior of the brand's leader.

Visionary leaders create a culture of innovation, creativity, and continuous learning, encouraging their teams to think outside the box and embrace new ideas. They empower others to reach their full potential, providing mentorship, coaching, and opportunities for growth and development. Visionary leaders navigate challenges and setbacks with resilience and determination, guiding their teams through periods of uncertainty and change. They build strong relationships with shareholders, customers, and partners, building trust, loyalty, and collaboration.

Ultimately, a Visionary leader serves as the soul of their brand or company by inspiring and empowering others to share in their passion and commitment and driving their brand to generational success. Here are several key ways in which Visionary leaders ensure the soul they epitomize is aligned with their vision:

Definitive Vision | A Visionary leader articulates a clear and compelling vision for the future of the brand or company. This vision is a guiding light, inspiring and aligning the team's efforts toward common goals and aspirations.

Building the Culture | Visionary leaders define and set the tone for the organization's culture, principles, and values. Their words and actions establish behavior, communication, and collaboration norms that reflect the brand's identity and ethos.

Relentless Innovation | Visionary leaders are relentless innovators and creators, constantly pushing the boundaries of what's possible and encouraging their team to think creatively. They build a culture of experimentation and risk-taking, where new ideas are a rite of passage and opportunities are nurtured.

Principles-Centered Leadership | Visionary leaders lead by example, manage through foundational principles, and embody the values and behaviors they wish to see in their team. They demonstrate integrity, authenticity, and a strong work ethic, inspiring trust and respect among their followers.

Inspiration | Visionary leaders inspire and motivate others with passion, enthusiasm, and unwavering belief in the organization's mission. They communicate their vision with clarity and conviction, rallying support and commitment from their team.

Growth Mindset | Visionary leaders invest in the growth and development of their team members, empowering them to reach their full potential. They provide mentorship, coaching, and opportunities for learning and advancement.

Overcoming Challenges | Visionary leaders navigate challenges and setbacks with resilience and determination, guiding their teams through periods of uncertainty and change. They remain steadfast in their commitment to the organization's mission, inspiring confidence and stability during turbulent times.

Building Relationships | Visionary leaders cultivate strong relationships with stakeholders, customers, and partners, fostering trust, loyalty, and collaboration. They prioritize open communication and transparency, building bridges and fostering goodwill within the community.

The Soul Requires Balance

When you're surrounded by people who share a passionate commitment around a common purpose, anything is possible.
– Howard Schultz

Visionary leaders who are the soul of their brand encounter many challenges as they strive to uphold their organization's essence, values, and vision. Being the soul of an organization is a delicate balancing act, requiring careful navigation of several different priorities at once.

One prominent leader widely regarded as a brand's soul is Howard Schultz, the former CEO and Chairman of Starbucks

Corporation. Schultz played a pivotal role in shaping Starbucks into the globally recognized brand it is today, embodying its values, vision, and mission throughout his tenure. Under Schultz's leadership, Starbucks expanded rapidly, becoming synonymous with premium coffee and the third place between work and home. Schultz's commitment to social responsibility and ethical business practices also defined his leadership at Starbucks. Also, Schultz's passion for innovation and customer experience drove Starbucks to explore new ventures beyond traditional coffee shops; he oversaw the expansion of the Starbucks brand into areas such as food products, mobile payments, and digital technology, continually adapting to changing consumer preferences and market trends.

Throughout his tenure at Starbucks, Schultz remained deeply connected to the brand's identity and values, earning him a reputation as the company's soul. Even after stepping down as CEO, Schultz continued to advocate for Starbucks and its mission, further solidifying his legacy as a Visionary leader who personified the essence of the Starbucks brand. In short, Schultz's priorities as a leader—expansion, ethics, innovation—grew into the soul of the company itself, characterized above all as an expansive, ethical, and innovative brand like none other.

One of the primary challenges to achieving balance in maintaining the soul of a brand is preserving authenticity during growth and expansion. As the brand evolves and scales, there's often pressure to compromise on core values or dilute the brand's identity to appeal to a broader audience. Managing growth can be daunting, requiring leaders to maintain organizational culture, ensure consistency across locations, and manage talent effectively. This challenge is compounded by the need to navigate change and uncertainty in a rapidly evolving business environment, anticipate trends, and make strategic decisions during constant disruption. The results of too-quick expansion are typically dire, as seen in the recent dissolution of flash-in-the-pan brands or chains that choose to surrender what made them beloved in pursuit of rapid expansion.

Striking a balance between innovation and tradition poses another significant challenge. Visionary leaders must drive innovation while honoring the traditions and heritage that define their brand, navigating the delicate tension between pushing boundaries and preserving what makes the brand unique. Staying relevant in the face of competition and managing the brand team and customer and community expectations also present ongoing challenges.

Along with being the heart and soul of a brand comes the challenge of sustainability and success. These Visionary leaders who are the soul of their brands maintain their successful track record by staying true to their core foundational principles, consistently embodying the core values and principles that define their organization while also adapting to changing circumstances and evolving market dynamics.

These Visionary leaders remain authentic to their brand's identity and heritage, ensuring that every decision and action aligns with the fundamental values guiding their success over generations. To that end, Visionary leaders empower and develop their teams, recognizing that their organization's success is built on the talent and dedication of its people. They invest in training, mentorship, and career development, creating an environment where employees feel valued, motivated, and empowered to contribute their best. Strategic partnerships and collaborations are also key to sustaining success, as Visionary leaders seek opportunities to leverage other organizations' strengths and expand their reach and impact.

Overall, navigating these challenges demands vision, creativity, adaptability, and unwavering commitment from Visionary leaders who serve as the soul of their brand.

Why Soul Matters

A Visionary leader who takes their job as the soul of their organization seriously must maintain a long-term perspective, making strategic decisions that position their organizations for sustainable growth and success despite short-term challenges or setbacks. Through their unwavering commitment to their vision, values, and people, Visionary leaders who are faithful souls of their brands continue to drive their organizations forward, building on their successful reputation and shaping the future of their industries.

Live. Engrain. Grow.

The Visionary | ELON MUSK

When something is important enough, you do it even if the odds are not in your favor.
– Elon Musk

Elon Musk is a Visionary leader, entrepreneur, and CEO who has founded and led companies such as Tesla, PayPal, SpaceX, Neuralink, and The Boring Company.

Musk was born on June 28, 1971, in Pretoria, South Africa, and has become one of the most prominent figures in the technology and space industries. Over the years, Musk has had a successful track record of disrupting traditional industries and introducing innovative solutions. Companies like Tesla and SpaceX have challenged established norms in the automotive and aerospace sectors, demonstrating Musk's commitment to pushing technological boundaries.

Musk's ventures span multiple industries, from electric vehicles and space exploration to renewable energy and neuroscience. His Visionary mindset marks his ability to leverage expertise across domains and integrate technologies, and he is known for his ambitious, futuristic, and insightful vision. His goals include colonizing Mars, transitioning the world to sustainable energy, advancing neural interfaces, and revolutionizing transportation. With his futuristic vision, Musk aims to address long-term challenges facing humanity.

These ambitious goals reflect his visionary insight. Musk is known for taking significant risks in pursuit of his goals. He embraces calculated risk-taking and is unafraid to challenge the status quo. From investing his money into SpaceX when faced with potential failure to pursuing challenging projects with significant risk, his resilience and perseverance set him apart as a Visionary leader. With a dynamic, futuristic vision, he invests heavily in future technologies with transformative potential. Ventures like Neuralink's brain–machine interface demonstrate his commitment to advancing technologies that could reshape industries and human capabilities. Musk's passion for innovation is a driving force behind his insight-driven strategies. His enthusiasm for exploring new ideas and pushing technological boundaries contributes to the success of his ventures.

Musk is actively involved in the development and innovation processes of his companies. This hands-on approach—whether in engineering, design, or problem-solving—reflects a deep commitment to the success of his ventures and emphasizes long-term thinking and planning. His focus on addressing these critical global challenges, such as climate change and interplanetary colonization, demonstrates a strategic and forward-looking perspective. Musk approaches problem-solving iteratively like other Visionaries, gaining insights from each iteration. Whether it's improving electric vehicle technology or optimizing space launch capabilities, he actively seeks solutions and continuously refines his approach based on insights gained from previous attempts.

Musk emphasizes long-term thinking and planning. His insight into the potential long-term impacts of his ventures influences decision-making and encourages investment in projects that may take years to yield results. Strategic planning is a core principle of Musk based on a comprehensive understanding of industry trends and competitive landscapes. His insight allows him to strategically position his companies, anticipate challenges, and identify opportunities. Musk's vision also extends globally. His ability to draw insights from engineering, physics, computer science, and business enables him to tackle complex challenges and integrate diverse technologies into cohesive solutions.

With companies like Tesla, Musk prioritizes customer needs and desires. He focuses on creating products that address environmental concerns and offer a superior user experience, demonstrating a customer-centric approach to innovation. Musk is dedicated to sustainability and environmental responsibility, and he aims to accelerate the world's transition to sustainable energy sources through Tesla's electric vehicles and solar energy initiatives. His initiatives in space exploration, renewable energy, and transportation have the potential to impact people worldwide, addressing both local and global challenges.

Musk is open to feedback and iteration, acknowledges mistakes, learns from failures and iterates on designs and strategies. Musk views setbacks as opportunities to learn and improve. His insight-driven approach involves analyzing failures, extracting valuable insights, and applying lessons learned to enhance future endeavors. This adaptability contributes to the ongoing success and improvement of his ventures.

Though his approach may sometimes flirt with controversy, it cannot be denied that Musk is an effective communicator adept at expressing his vision to the public. His use of social media, public appearances, and brand communication contributes to building excitement and support for his ventures, creating a strong public perception of his ventures. Musk maintains open communication with investors, employees, and the media. His insights into the progress and challenges of his companies are often shared transparently, creating a level of trust and understanding within the stakeholder community.

In summary, Elon Musk's Visionary insights include his **ambitious vision for the future**, a **passion for innovation and disruption**, **risk-taking and resilience**, **hands-on leadership**, **long-term thinking**, **effective public communication**, **investment in future technologies**, and a **global impact**. His influence extends across various industries, making him a prominent visionary in technology and entrepreneurship. His work has earned him recognition as one of the most influential people in the world, and he continues to play a pivotal role in shaping the future of technology and sustainability.

ACCOMPLISHMENTS

PayPal | Musk co-founded X.com, an online payment company, in 1999. X.com later became PayPal after a merger, and in 2002, it was acquired by eBay for $1.5 billion in stock. PayPal revolutionized online payments, making secure transactions accessible to millions of users.

Tesla | Musk co-founded Tesla, Inc. in 2003, aspiring to accelerate the world's transition to sustainable energy. Tesla pioneered electric vehicles (EVs) and renewable energy solutions. Under Musk's leadership, Tesla produced revolutionary electric cars, including the Model S, Model 3, Model X, and Model Y, making EVs more mainstream and transforming the automotive industry.

SpaceX | In 2002, Musk founded Space Exploration Technologies Corp. (SpaceX) to reduce space transportation costs and enable human colonization of Mars. SpaceX developed the Falcon 1, Falcon 9, Falcon Heavy rockets, and Dragon spacecraft. The company achieved multiple historic milestones, including the first privately funded spacecraft to reach orbit and the first privately funded spacecraft to dock with the International Space Station (ISS).

SolarCity | Musk co-founded SolarCity in 2006, a company that produces solar energy products and services. SolarCity intended to make solar energy more accessible to homeowners and businesses. The company was later acquired by Tesla, and its technology contributed to Tesla's solar products, including solar roofs and solar panels.

Hyperloop and The Boring Company | Musk proposed the concept of the Hyperloop, a high-speed transportation system using pressurized capsules in near-vacuum tubes. Although only partially realized, the idea sparked innovation and research in the transportation sector. Additionally, Musk founded The Boring Company, which focused on tunnel construction and infrastructure to reduce traffic congestion through underground transportation networks.

Neuralink | In 2016, Musk co-founded Neuralink, a neurotechnology company that develops brain-machine interfaces. The company's goal is to merge the human brain with artificial intelligence (AI) to enhance human cognitive abilities and address potential future challenges posed by advanced AI.

OpenAI | Musk co-founded OpenAI, an artificial intelligence research lab, in 2015. OpenAI aims to ensure that artificial general intelligence (AGI) benefits all of humanity. The organization conducts research, shares findings, and promotes cooperation in AI.

Chapter 14 | THE LONELINESS

The eternal quest of the individual human being
is to shatter his loneliness.

– Norman Cousins

Visionary leaders often experience a sense of loneliness as they navigate the journey of executing their vision. This loneliness stems from their unique challenges and responsibilities in charting a new course for their brand or disrupting an industry. Visionary leaders are often tasked with the daunting venture of transforming dreams into reality. They possess an unwavering belief in their vision and a relentless determination to see it through. As they embark on this solitary path, they may encounter a profound sense of loneliness. The weight of responsibility rests heavily upon their shoulders, and making tough decisions can be isolating.

Yet as negative a connotation as loneliness may have in our society, it is within this solitude that Visionary leaders find their strength. They draw upon their inner resilience and courage to navigate the inevitable challenges. They seek solace in their unwavering belief and the knowledge that they are blazing a trail for others to follow.

This loneliness can also catalyze personal growth. Visionary leaders push beyond their comfort zones, learning to rely on their instincts and convictions. They develop a deep understanding of themselves and their capabilities, empowering them to inspire and motivate those around them.

Loneliness Is Empowering

Why are Visionaries prone to loneliness? Ironically, the very characteristics that make them so special also set them apart from their fellow industry leaders. A leader who is consumed by their passion, who possesses unique insight into human minds and needs, who is burdened with acting as the soul of their organization and carrying the torch into the future—this person others may have a hard time relating to. Just as importantly, with so much on their plate, a Visionary frequently doesn't have much time to invest in personal relationships, which can leave them in a state of isolation.

At the heart of this loneliness is the Visionary leader's distinctive perspective and ambitious vision for the future, which may set them apart from their peers and team. They may find themselves grappling with decisions others may need help understanding or supporting, leading to isolation in their leadership role. Additionally, the weight of responsibility for driving the organization forward and delivering on their vision can be overwhelming, creating a sense of solitude in shouldering the burden of leadership.

Unfortunately, Visionary leaders often have a pressing need to be understood, and this need is uniquely hard to fill precisely due to their special Visionary qualities. Their ideas can be radical and challenging, and finding others who truly comprehend their vision can be difficult. This can lead to feelings of alienation and feeling alone in their endeavors.

Even with the support of their team and loved ones, Visionary leaders may still feel a sense of solitude in bearing the ultimate responsibility for the success or failure of their vision. However, it's essential for Visionary leaders to recognize and address these feelings of loneliness, seeking support from trusted supporters, mentors, and peers who can provide guidance, understanding, and encouragement along the journey. By acknowledging and coping with their loneliness, Visionary leaders can better navigate the challenges of executing their vision while maintaining their well-being and resilience.

Despite these challenges, Visionary leaders can find solace in knowing their solitude is necessary to realize their journey. In these moments of quiet contemplation, they can connect with their inner selves and find the strength and determination to continue their pursuit of a better future.

Visionary leaders recognize that authentic leadership is not about seeking recognition or glory. It is about making a meaningful contribution to the world. They find solace in knowing their legacy will live long after they are gone, inspiring future generations to dream big and strive for a better tomorrow.

Visionary leaders often find themselves isolated in their pursuit of extraordinary goals. Their path is often uncharted, and their weight of responsibility can be immense. This solitude can stem from several main factors:

Unique Perspective | Visionary leaders often have a unique perspective and vision for the future that others may not share. This can lead to isolation, as they may need help finding others who fully understand or support their vision.

Decision-Making Burden | Visionary leaders bear the burden of making tough decisions and charting the course for their organization's future. This responsibility can be isolating, as they may feel the weight of the decisions resting solely on their shoulders.

Lack of Peers | Visionary leaders may lack peers or colleagues who relate to their experiences and challenges. This can make it difficult to find support or guidance from others who understand Visionary leadership's unique pressures and responsibilities.

High Expectations | Visionary leaders are often expected to deliver results and achieve success. This pressure can contribute to loneliness, as they may feel they must constantly prove themselves and live up to others' expectations.

Sacrifices | Executing a vision often requires sacrifices, whether it's time away from family and friends, personal interests, or other aspects of life. These sacrifices can lead to isolation and loneliness as Visionary leaders prioritize their vision above other aspects of their lives.

In Visionary leadership, loneliness can be a constant shadow, a silent companion that lingers continually in their minds. As they start on their journey of bringing their extraordinary visions to realization, Visionary leaders often find themselves standing at a crossroads where solitude becomes an essential part of their path.

The weight of their aspirations and the insightful nature of their dreams can create a chasm between them and others, leaving them with a profound sense of isolation.

But remember, with challenge comes the opportunity for growth and, ultimately, strength. Within their solitude, Visionary leaders discover the depth of their resilience, the unwavering strength of their convictions, and the transformative power of their dreams. When others rest, the Visionary leader presses ahead. When doubt creeps in, the Visionary leader stands firm. They see possibilities while others see obstacles, and that gulf can create an isolating abyss.

Yes, it is in this solitude that the Visionary leader finds strength. The Visionary path is a lonely path, one where the weight of the vision falls heavily upon their minds. However, true leadership is not about popularity or conformity but about conviction and purpose, and the Visionary leader finds the clarity and resolve to carry on in quiet moments of reflection far from the crowds.

Loneliness Is Curable

Despite the loneliness that Visionary leaders may experience, they must find ways to cope with these feelings and seek support when needed. A leader who is suffering is not producing their best work; as the saying goes, you need to put the oxygen mask on yourself before you can help others.

Delegating responsibilities and empowering team members to take ownership of various aspects of the vision and strategy can alleviate some of the pressure and loneliness of leadership.

Cultivating meaningful relationships both inside and outside the workplace is also crucial for combating loneliness. By prioritizing self-care, maintaining a strong connection to their purpose and values, and celebrating achievements along the journey, Visionary leaders can overcome loneliness and lead their company with resilience, inspiration, and well-being.

Visionary leaders can take several steps to overcome the adverse effects of loneliness and maintain their well-being while leading their brand:

Support Network | Surround yourself with trusted advisors, mentors, and peers who understand the challenges of Visionary leadership. Look for focused networking opportunities, events, and leadership forums where you can connect with like-minded individuals and gain valuable insights and support.

Delegate Responsibilities | Recognize that you don't have to shoulder the burden of leadership alone. Whenever possible, delegate responsibilities and empower your team to take ownership of various aspects of the vision and strategy. By sharing the workload and fostering a sense of shared responsibility, you can alleviate some of the pressure and loneliness of leadership.

Meaningful Relationships | Invest time and effort into cultivating meaningful relationships inside and outside the workplace. Build strong connections with your team members, fostering a culture of collaboration, trust, and open communication. Outside of work, prioritize spending time with family, friends, and loved ones who provide emotional support and companionship.

Self-Preservation | Make self-care a priority in your daily routine. Take breaks when needed, engage in activities that bring you joy and relaxation, and prioritize your physical and mental well-being. Regular exercise, meditation, and mindfulness practices can help reduce stress and promote overall health and resilience.

Seek Professional Support | Don't hesitate to seek professional support if you're struggling with feelings of loneliness or being overwhelmed. Consider working with a coach, therapist, or counselor who can provide guidance, perspective, and coping strategies to help you navigate the challenges of Visionary leadership.

Stay Committed to Your Purpose | Remind yourself of the purpose and passion that drives your vision. Stay connected to your values, mission, and long-term goals, and draw inspiration from the impact you're striving to create. Connecting to your purpose can provide a sense of meaning and fulfillment, helping to combat feelings of loneliness and isolation.

Celebrate Achievements | Take time to celebrate milestones, achievements, and successes along the journey. Recognize and appreciate your progress, and acknowledge your team's contributions in bringing the vision to life. Celebrating achievements fosters a sense of camaraderie and shared accomplishment, strengthening bonds and combating feelings of loneliness.

Build Your Faith | Continue to find peace and commitment to growing your faith. Find ways to connect and read words that are spiritually important to you to find inspiration during trials and aspirations for the goals ahead.

By proactively addressing feelings of loneliness and prioritizing self-care, connection, and support, Visionary leaders can overcome the challenges of leading their company with resilience, purpose, and well-being.

Why Loneliness Matters

As a Visionary leader, forging a path to lasting success for your company and teams can be an isolating journey. But know this: within you lies a formidable force capable of overcoming loneliness and propelling you towards success.

Embrace the solitude that comes with being an innovator. In these quiet moments, your vision crystallizes and your leadership grows more potent. Seek solace in knowing that your path, though traveled alone, leads to a destination that will benefit many. Cultivate deep connections with a select few who truly understand your aspirations. These confidants will provide unwavering support and serve as a sounding board for your ideas. Remember, true companionship is not found in the masses but in the quality of the relationships you build.

Don't hide your loneliness, but lead with authenticity and vulnerability. Sharing your struggles and aspirations creates a space where others feel seen and understood. This fosters a culture of trust and solidarity, breaking down the barriers that can lead to isolation. Recognize that your team is not merely a collection of individuals but diverse perspectives. Encourage their input and ideas, valuing each voice as a vital bloodline in the heart and soul of your vision. Authentic leadership empowers others and creates a sense of shared purpose that transcends feelings of isolation.

Most of all, never lose sight of your "why." The unwavering belief in your mission and its impact on the world will sustain you through moments of loneliness. Remember that your vision is for personal gain and the betterment of all you lead. Embrace solitude, cultivate meaningful connections, and stay grounded in your purpose. By doing this, you will overcome loneliness and forge an unbreakable bond with those who follow you, propelling your company and teams to remarkable success.

Isolate. Delegate. Energize.

The Visionary | LUDWIG VAN BEETHOVEN

Music is the mediator between the spiritual and the sensual life.
– Ludwig van Beethoven

Ludwig van Beethoven (1770–1827) was a German composer and pianist widely regarded as one of the greatest composers in Western classical music history. Triumphs and struggles marked his life, mainly stemming from his solitude, and the music produced through these difficult times continues to inspire and captivate audiences worldwide.

Beethoven was born in Bonn, Germany, into a musical family. His father, Johann van Beethoven, was a singer and musician, and he recognized his son's musical talent at an early age. Beethoven received his early music education from his father and other local teachers. He gave his first public performance at seven and soon gained a reputation as a child prodigy.

In his early adulthood, Beethoven moved to Vienna, the musical capital of Europe, to study with renowned composers such as Joseph Haydn and Wolfgang Amadeus Mozart. He quickly established himself as a virtuoso pianist and composer, gaining the patronage of aristocrats and earning a living through composing, performing, and teaching music.

Beethoven's early works were influenced by the classical style of his predecessors, Haydn and Mozart, but he soon began to develop his own distinctive voice as a composer. He experimented with form, structure, and expression, pushing the boundaries of musical convention and paving the way for the Romantic era of music. His Visionary compositions anticipated the shifts that would define the musical landscape in the 19th century.

Beethoven's music is known for its emotional depth and expressiveness. He infused his compositions with intense emotions, creating a more personal and subjective connection between the composer and the listener. This emotional resonance paved the way for the Romantic emphasis on individual expression.

Beethoven also demonstrated a strong sense of individualism in his approach to composition. Unlike many of his equals, who often composed at the behest of patrons or aristocrats, Beethoven pursued his artistic vision independently, prioritizing his creative instincts over external expectations.

Perhaps Beethoven's most significant achievements were his nine symphonies, which revolutionized the genre and expanded the possibilities of orchestral music. His *Symphony No. 3 in E-flat major*, also known as the "Eroica," marked a turning point in symphonic composition with its grand scale, emotional depth, and innovative use of musical motifs. "Eroica" was initially dedicated to Napoleon Bonaparte and embodied the ideals of heroism and the pursuit of freedom, making it a characteristically revolutionary composition by Beethoven.

Throughout his life, Beethoven faced numerous personal challenges, including deteriorating hearing, eventually leaving him completely deaf. Despite this obstacle, he continued to compose music of unparalleled beauty and complexity, relying on his inner musical imagination to create some of his greatest masterpieces. His music is characterized by its emotional intensity, innovative harmonies, and thoughtful expression of human emotion.

Beethoven was known for his intense and passionate personality, which could sometimes lead to feelings of isolation and alienation from others. One significant factor contributing to Beethoven's sense of isolation and sometimes loneliness was his increasing deafness, which began manifesting in his late 20s and eventually left him profoundly deaf by his mid-40s. This loss of hearing deeply affected his ability to communicate and interact with others, leading to feelings of loneliness and frustration.

Additionally, Beethoven faced various personal and emotional challenges throughout his life, including strained relationships with family members, unrequited love, and financial difficulties.

These struggles undoubtedly contributed to periods of loneliness and isolation.

However, despite his disability, Beethoven also maintained meaningful relationships and connections with others, including close friendships with fellow musicians, patrons, and supporters. He found support and companionship in his music, which served as a source of expression and connection with audiences despite his deafness.

While Beethoven may have experienced loneliness at times, particularly during periods of personal and professional turmoil, his life was also filled with moments of creativity, passion, and human connection that transcended feelings of isolation. Indeed, in many ways, his loneliness may well have fueled some of his greatest artistic achievements, allowing Beethoven to retreat into an interior space where he could compose his music without interruptions.

Beethoven's music continues to be celebrated for its emotional depth, innovation, and enduring appeal, making him one of the most influential composers in the history of classical music. His music continues to inspire and resonate with audiences worldwide, a testament to the enduring power of his Visionary genius.

Ludwig van Beethoven's Visionary characteristics include **innovation, emotional depth, individualism and autonomy, innovative use of form and structure, resilience in the face of adversity, a revolutionary spirit, exploration of unconventional elements**, and **maintaining his vision in the face of isolation and loneliness**.

ACCOMPLISHMENTS

Musical Innovation | Beethoven's compositions were groundbreaking and innovative, marking a transition from the classical style to the Romantic period. His ability to push the boundaries of musical conventions and experiment with form, structure, and expression set him apart as a Visionary in the evolution of music.

Symphonic Innovation | Beethoven's symphonies, particularly the Ninth Symphony with its choral finale, expanded the possibilities of the symphonic form. The inclusion of voices in the final movement was an innovative departure from traditional symphonic structure and contributed to the work's lasting impact. His *Symphony No. 3 in E-flat major, Op. 55*, also known as the "Eroica Symphony," marked a turning point in the history of classical music due to its innovative structure and emotional depth.

Innovative Use of Form and Structure | Beethoven expanded the traditional forms of classical music, introducing innovations in sonata-allegro form, symphonic structure, and thematic development. His compositions, particularly in his later works, exhibit a departure from classical norms, displaying a forward-looking and Visionary approach to musical structure.

Piano Sonatas | Beethoven composed 32 piano sonatas, showcasing his innovation and mastery of the form. His "Moonlight Sonata" (*Piano Sonata No. 14 in C-sharp minor, Op. 27, No. 2*) is one of the world's most famous and frequently performed piano compositions.

Unconventional Harmonies and Rhythms | Beethoven's use of unconventional harmonies, rhythmic complexities, and dynamic contrasts challenged the norms of his time. His willingness to explore new harmonic and rhythmic territories contributed to the visionary character of his music.

String Quartets | Beethoven composed a set of 16 string quartets, considered some of the finest works in the chamber music repertoire. His late string quartets, including the profound and introspective *String Quartet No. 14 in C-sharp minor, Op. 131*, are mainly celebrated for their complexity and emotional depth.

Piano Concertos | Beethoven composed five piano concertos, revolutionizing the piano concerto genre. His *Piano Concerto No. 5 in E-flat major, Op. 73*, also known as the "Emperor Concerto," is renowned for its grandeur and virtuosity.

Opera | While Beethoven composed only one opera, "Fidelio," it is considered a triumph of the human spirit. The opera explores themes of freedom, justice, and the power of love with beautiful arias and dramatic orchestration.

Overtures | Beethoven composed several iconic overtures, including the stirring overture to "Egmont," Op. 84, and the jubilant "Leonore Overture No. 3," Op. 72a, both of which are frequently performed in concert halls around the world.

Choral Works | In addition to his Ninth Symphony, Beethoven composed other choral works, such as the *Mass in C major, Op. 86*, and the "Missa Solemnis," Op. 123. These compositions showcase his mastery of large-scale choral writing.

Chapter 15 | THE FAITH

Faith consists in believing when it is beyond the power of reason to believe.

– Voltaire

Visionary leaders often rely on faith as a guiding force to accomplish their vision. This faith may manifest in various forms, including belief in themselves, their vision, their team, and something greater than themselves. At the core of their faith is a deep conviction in the possibility of realizing their vision, even in the face of uncertainty, doubt, and adversity. This unwavering belief fuels their persistence, resilience, and determination, allowing them to persevere through challenges and setbacks.

Visionary leaders draw strength from their faith, trusting that their efforts will yield positive outcomes and that their vision has the power to make a meaningful impact. Also, faith instills a sense of purpose and meaning in their work, anchoring them to their values and inspiring them to lead with integrity, passion, and compassion. By embracing faith as a guiding principle, Visionary leaders tap into infinite inner strength and courage, empowering them to boldly pursue their vision and bring about transformative change in their companies and beyond.

Faith Is Powerful

Applied faith has been instrumental in helping Visionary leaders navigate tough times and ultimately achieve success by providing them with an inner sense of purpose. During challenging moments such as facing setbacks, criticism, or uncertainty, Visionary leaders draw upon their faith to maintain optimism and determination. Their belief in the validity of their vision, coupled with a trust in themselves and their team, sustains them through adversity, enabling them to persevere when others might fail.

Applied faith also fosters a mindset of infinite possibility, allowing leaders to view obstacles as opportunities for growth and learning rather than overwhelming barriers. By remaining loyal to their faith, Visionary leaders inspire confidence and commitment in their team, uniting them around a shared sense of purpose and conviction. Over time, this unwavering belief in their vision and ability to overcome trials propels Visionary leaders forward, guiding them toward success and fulfilling their aspirations. Applied faith is a guiding light illuminating the path through tough times, leading Visionary leaders toward their ultimate triumphs.

Leaders can embrace faith daily by integrating spiritual principles into their personal and professional routines. This involves cultivating a mindset rooted in trust, belief, and purpose, which can positively impact their decision-making, relationships, and overall well-being.

First, leaders can start each day with moments of reflection, meditation, or prayer to center themselves and connect with their inner beliefs and values. Setting intentions aligned with their core principles can provide a sense of clarity and direction for the day ahead. Leaders can practice gratitude throughout the day, acknowledging the blessings and opportunities present in their lives, even amidst challenges. They can approach interactions with compassion, empathy, and humility, recognizing every individual's inherent worth and dignity.

Additionally, leaders can seek inspiration from their faith traditions, scriptures, or spiritual teachings, drawing strength and guidance from these sources in times of uncertainty or adversity. By infusing their daily lives with faith, leaders can cultivate a sense of peace, purpose, and resilience, enabling them to navigate challenges with grace and authenticity while inspiring those around them.

History is full of Visionaries who have navigated adversity's treacherous waters with the unwavering compass of faith. From adversity to triumph, their journeys are testaments to the indomitable human spirit when fortified by a deep-seated connection to a higher purpose. In the depths of despair, faith empowers these leaders to see beyond the immediate storm, igniting a hope that guides them toward unwavering resilience. It provides an inner fortitude that steels their resolve, enabling them to persevere through challenges that would otherwise break them. Furthermore, faith nurtures a sense of peace and tranquility amidst the chaos of uncertainty. When the path ahead seems dark, it sheds light upon their steps, showing the way forward with clarity and purpose. It empowers them to embrace failure as a stepping stone toward growth and to recognize setbacks as opportunities for refinement.

Through applied faith, Visionary leaders tap into a strength that transcends explanation. They draw upon their spiritual beliefs to find meaning and purpose in adversity, knowing their challenges are chapters in a grander narrative. Faith empowers them to embrace failure as a necessary teacher, a catalyst for growth and innovation. It fuels their determination to rise above obstacles, learn from their mistakes, and emerge stronger.

Finally, faith fosters a mindset of gratitude, enabling leaders to appreciate the blessings amidst the challenges. They recognize that even in the most trying of times, there is always something to be grateful for, a source of strength to draw upon. With faith as their compass, Visionary leaders navigate the treacherous terrain of adversity with confidence and resolve. They know they are not alone and that a higher power is guiding their steps. This empowers them to make bold decisions, take calculated risks, and lead their teams toward uncharted territories.

Several Visionary leaders throughout history have demonstrated a strong faith that guided their actions and fueled the pursuit of their vision. In addition to Dr. Martin Luther King Jr., whom we will study in greater detail below, here are just a few examples of generational faith-centered Visionary leaders:

You must not lose faith in humanity. Humanity is an ocean;
if a few drops of the ocean are dirty, the ocean does not
become dirty.
– Mahatma Gandhi

Mahatma Gandhi | Gandhi, the leader of the Indian independence movement against British rule, was deeply influenced by his faith in nonviolence (*ahimsa*) and truth (*satyagraha*). His spiritual beliefs, rooted in Hinduism, Jainism, and Christianity, shaped his commitment to social justice, equality, and nonviolent resistance. Gandhi's unwavering faith in the power of love and compassion inspired millions and played a pivotal role in India's struggle for independence, and we will learn more from this Visionary in the next chapter.

We need to find God, and he cannot be found in noise and restlessness. God is the friend of silence. See how nature—trees, flowers, grass—grows in silence; see the stars, the moon and the sun, how they move in silence... We need silence to be able to touch souls.
– Mother Teresa

Mother Teresa | Mother Teresa, known for her humanitarian work and dedication to serving the poor and sick in Calcutta, India, exemplified a profound faith in action. As a Catholic nun and missionary, she viewed her service to the marginalized and suffering as a manifestation of her love for God. Mother Teresa's unwavering commitment to compassion, humility, and selflessness, rooted in her Catholic faith, earned her widespread admiration and recognition, including the Nobel Peace Prize in 1979.

It always seems impossible until it's done.
– Nelson Mandela

Nelson Mandela | Nelson Mandela, the anti-apartheid revolutionary and former president of South Africa, drew on his faith in justice, reconciliation, and forgiveness during his decades-long struggle against apartheid. Mandela's upbringing in the Methodist Church and his belief in all people's inherent dignity and equality informed his vision of a democratic and multiracial South Africa. Despite enduring 27 years of imprisonment, Mandela remained steadfast in his commitment to peace, reconciliation, and building a unified nation.

These Visionary leaders exemplify how faith can serve as a powerful force for inspiration, resilience, and transformative change, shaping their vision and guiding their actions in pursuing a better world.

Faith Is Indispensable

Visionaries who embrace faith as an integral part of their leadership journey harness its transformative power to overcome barriers to success and emerge stronger. They find solace and strength in the most trying times by aligning their goals with a higher purpose and drawing inspiration from spiritual principles.

Faith empowers Visionaries to embrace adversity as a catalyst for growth. They understand that setbacks are opportunities to refine their vision, develop their character, and deepen their understanding of the world. By trusting in their unrelenting faith, they cultivate an unshakeable belief that, ultimately, their efforts will bear fruit. Also, applied faith builds a sense of community and shared purpose among Visionary leaders. They recognize that their success is intertwined with the well-being of others, and they are driven by a desire to create positive change in the world. By uniting under common values and aspirations, they form an insurmountable force that can overcome any obstacle.

Visionary leaders often utilize faith as a powerful tool to propel them forward in accomplishing their vision. Faith, in this context, encompasses a belief in oneself, in the vision itself, and in the process of achieving it. Here's how Visionary leaders harness faith:

Belief in Self | Visionary leaders have a deep-seated belief in their ability to realize their vision. This self-confidence enables them to face challenges and setbacks with resilience, knowing they have the skills and determination to overcome obstacles.

Belief in the Vision | Visionary leaders unwaveringly believe in the validity and importance of their vision. They clearly understand their vision's impact and remain steadfast in their commitment to bringing it to fruition, even when others may doubt its feasibility or significance.

Belief in the Process | Visionary leaders trust in their ability to achieve their vision, recognizing that success often requires patience, persistence, and perseverance. They have faith that each step taken, even in the face of uncertainty, contributes to realizing their ultimate goal.

Drawing Strength from Adversity | In moments of doubt or adversity, Visionary leaders rely on their faith to navigate challenges. They view setbacks as opportunities for growth and learning, drawing strength from their belief in their ability to overcome obstacles and emerge stronger on the other side.

Inspiring Others | Visionary leaders inspire confidence and commitment in others by embodying faith in themselves and their vision. Their unwavering belief and optimism are contagious, rallying their team members and stakeholders around a shared sense of purpose and possibility.

Staying Resilient | Faith empowers Visionary leaders to stay resilient despite uncertainty and ambiguity. They remain focused on their long-term vision, trusting that their efforts will yield results over time, even when immediate outcomes may be uncertain.

Overall, faith serves as a cornerstone for Visionary leaders, providing them with the inner strength, resilience, and optimism needed to persevere in pursuing their vision and ultimately bring about meaningful change in their organizations and the world. Faith propels them forward, empowering them to transcend limitations. They recognize the synergy between earthly actions and godly inspiration. Each day, they set aside time for reflection, seeking divine wisdom to infuse their endeavors with purpose and clarity.

Faith becomes an unwavering principle in the lives of Visionary leaders, grounding them amidst the turbulence of uncertainty. It fuels their resolve to persevere, transforming challenges into steps toward achieving their vision. Through prayer and meditation, they cultivate a deep connection to the source of all possibilities, unlocking hidden potential and innovative solutions.

Faith empowers Visionary Leaders to embrace uncertainty,

believing every obstacle holds the seeds of new opportunities. It inspires them to lead with courage and compassion, recognizing that a higher power guides their actions and reminding them that even the grandest of visions can be realized through unwavering belief.

Why Faith Matters

Ultimately, applied faith transforms Visionary leaders into bonfires of hope and inspiration. Their unwavering belief empowers others to overcome obstacles and strive for greatness. They leave a lasting legacy of resilience, innovation, and triumph, proving that even in the face of adversity, the power of faith can lead to extraordinary achievements.

Therefore, let's not underestimate the profound impact that applied faith can have on the journeys of Visionary leaders. It is not merely a personal conviction but a potent force that empowers them to navigate adversity, inspire others, and create a lasting legacy of positive change.

So, to the Visionary leaders who dare to dream and the courageous souls who blaze new trails: let faith be your guide, your unwavering companion, and the source of your triumph. In its embrace, you will discover the strength to weather life's storms and emerge triumphant. Commit now to following other Visionary leaders who have harnessed the transformative power of applied faith. Let it guide you through tough times, ignite your passions, and propel you towards extraordinary achievements.

Believe. Achieve. Thrive.

The Visionary | DR. MARTIN LUTHER KING JR.

Faith is taking the first step even when you don't see the whole staircase.
– Dr. Martin Luther King Jr.

Dr. Martin Luther King Jr. was an iconic, Visionary leader in the American civil rights movement, known for his advocacy of nonviolent protest and his role in advancing civil rights and social justice for African Americans. He is also a powerful example of how faith can transform an individual's life and, in the hands of a Visionary, the very face of a nation.

Dr. King was born in a deeply religious family in Atlanta, Georgia, on January 15, 1929, and excelled academically. He earned a bachelor's degree in sociology from Morehouse College in 1948, a Bachelor of Divinity degree from Crozer Theological Seminary in 1951, and a Ph.D. in systematic theology from Boston University in 1955.

Dr. King's involvement in the civil rights movement began in the mid-1950s when he led the Montgomery Bus Boycott, sparked by Rosa Parks' arrest for refusing to give up her seat on a segregated bus. His leadership during the boycott catapulted him to national prominence and established him as a leading voice in the struggle for racial equality. Throughout the late 1950s and early 1960s, Dr. King advocated for civil rights through nonviolent resistance and civil disobedience. He helped organize the Southern Christian Leadership Conference (SCLC) in 1957. He served as its first president, using the organization as a platform to coordinate nonviolent protests and campaigns across the South.

One of Dr. King's most iconic moments came during the March on Washington for Jobs and Freedom in 1963, where he delivered his famous "I Have a Dream" speech to a crowd of over 250,000 people gathered at the Lincoln Memorial. The speech called for an end to racism and discrimination and remains one of the most celebrated and influential speeches in American history.

In 1964, Dr. King was awarded the Nobel Peace Prize for his leadership in the civil rights movement. Throughout the remainder of the 1960s, he advocated for racial justice, leading nationwide marches, boycotts, and demonstrations.

Tragically, Dr. Martin Luther King Jr. was assassinated on April 4, 1968, in Memphis, Tennessee, where he had traveled to support striking sanitation workers. His death sparked outrage and mourning across the nation, but his legacy as a champion of civil rights and nonviolent protest continues to inspire generations of activists and leaders worldwide.

In every respect, Dr. King exemplified the application of faith in his civil rights movement leadership. Rooted deeply in his Christian beliefs, King's approach to leadership was filled with principles of love, justice, and nonviolence. The concept of applied faith was central to his philosophy, which guided his actions and inspired those around him. He saw himself as a moral leader called to uphold the principles of justice, equality, and dignity for all people, regardless of race. His faith provided him with the conviction and courage to challenge systemic racism and segregation, even in the face of violence and opposition.

King believed fervently in the power of love to overcome hatred and injustice, and he preached a message of nonviolent resistance to achieve social change. Drawing on the teachings of Jesus Christ, King urged his followers to respond to violence with love, to hate with understanding, and to injustice with righteousness. His faith gave him the moral authority to challenge segregation and discrimination, even in adversity. Dr. King's speeches and sermons were infused with biblical imagery and themes, inspiring hope and unity among his followers and galvanizing support for the civil rights movement.

Dr. King demonstrated personal sacrifice and humility throughout his leadership, willingly enduring hardship and persecution for justice and equality. He endured numerous hardships, including arrests, threats, and physical attacks, yet he remained steadfast in his dedication to the cause of civil rights. His willingness to sacrifice his safety and comfort for the greater good inspired others to join the movement and follow his example. His unwavering commitment to nonviolence and his steadfast belief in the moral arc of the universe bending towards justice served as a beacon of hope for millions, and his legacy continues to inspire generations.

Dr. King's work was deeply rooted in his Christian faith, and he consistently applied his faith-driven principles in his civil rights movement leadership. He appealed to shared values and beliefs, emphasizing the common humanity of all people and the possibility of achieving racial harmony and justice. His message of hope, rooted in his faith, resonated deeply with audiences and galvanized support for the civil rights movement.

Over his lifetime, Dr. Martin Luther King Jr. exemplified applied faith in his civil rights movement leadership, drawing on his Christian beliefs to inspire nonviolent resistance, assert moral authority, inspire hope and unity, demonstrate personal sacrifice, and advocate for forgiveness and reconciliation. His faith provided the moral foundation for his leadership and continues to inspire activists and leaders worldwide.

Over and above the prevailing power of his faith, Dr. King's vision was made possible through other Visionary traits. For one thing, King was inarguably a charismatic and eloquent speaker. His ability to communicate complex ideas in a way that resonated with a broad audience helped mobilize support for the civil rights movement. His speeches and writings continue to be admired for their rhetorical power.

He was also a strategic leader who understood the importance of planning and organization. His leadership in organizing protests, boycotts, and marches, such as the Montgomery Bus Boycott and the March on Washington, demonstrated his strategic insight. Dr. King believed in an inclusive approach to leadership that welcomed individuals from diverse backgrounds and communities. He sought to build alliances and coalitions to amplify the impact of the civil rights movement.

Dr. King's indomitable spirit propelled him to challenge the oppressive systems of his time fearlessly. His speeches, brimming with eloquence and passion, ignited a fire in the hearts of countless individuals, galvanizing them to join his fight for civil rights. He walked with unwavering courage in the face of adversity, demonstrating that one person's determination can move mountains.

Dr. King's leadership was not about personal glory but about empowering others. He believed that everyone had the potential to make a difference, and he tirelessly nurtured the growth of community leaders within the civil rights movement. His servant-oriented approach fostered a sense of collective ownership and responsibility, ensuring the movement's long-term success.

Dr. Martin Luther King Jr.'s Visionary leadership was characterized by his **unwavering courage**, **moral clarity**, **strategic thinking**, **servant-oriented approach**, **inclusivity**, **charismatic communication**, **long-term vision**, and **deep spiritual conviction**. These qualities enabled him to articulate a compelling vision of a just and equitable society and to inspire millions to join him in the fight for its realization. King's legacy as a Visionary leader continues to guide and inspire us today, reminding us of the transformative power of courage, compassion, and determination.

ACCOMPLISHMENTS

Civil Rights Leadership | Dr. Martin Luther King Jr. played a central role in the American civil rights movement of the 1950s and 1960s. He was a charismatic and inspirational leader who advocated for racial equality and justice.

Montgomery Bus Boycott (1955-1956) | Dr. King emerged as a leader during the Montgomery Bus Boycott, a year-long protest against racial segregation on public buses in Montgomery, Alabama. The boycott led to a Supreme Court decision declaring segregation on public buses unconstitutional.

Southern Christian Leadership Conference (SCLC) | Dr. King co-founded the SCLC in 1957, an organization committed to nonviolent protest and civil rights activism. He served as the organization's first president and used it as a platform for advocating for civil rights.

March on Washington for Jobs and Freedom (1963) | Dr. King delivered his famous "I Have a Dream" speech during the March on Washington, a historic event attended by thousands. This speech remains one of history's most iconic and influential calls for racial equality and civil rights.

Civil Rights Act of 1964 | Dr. King's leadership and advocacy played a crucial role in the passage of this Congressional act, which outlawed racial segregation and discrimination in public facilities and employment.

Voting Rights Act of 1965 | Dr. King's efforts, along with those of other civil rights activists, were instrumental in the passage of the Voting Rights Act of 1965. This legislation aimed to eliminate racial barriers to voting, particularly in the South.

Nobel Peace Prize (1964) | Martin Luther King Jr. was awarded the Nobel Peace Prize in 1964 for his nonviolent activism in the struggle for civil rights and his commitment to promoting social justice and racial equality.

Legacy of Nonviolent Protest | Dr. King's commitment to and philosophy of nonviolent civil disobedience inspired civil rights movements worldwide. His approach was a model for future social justice and human rights movements.

Advocacy for Economic Justice | Besides civil rights, King advocated for economic justice and was a vocal critic of economic inequality. He believed that addressing poverty and inequality was integral to achieving racial equality.

Generational Influence | Martin Luther King Jr.'s message and legacy continue to influence generations of activists and leaders committed to social justice, civil rights, and equality. His birthday is celebrated as a national holiday in the United States, and his name is synonymous with the fight for civil rights.

Chapter 16 | THE DEDICATION

Not life, but a good life, is to be chiefly valued.

– Socrates

Visionaries who dedicate their lives to their core principles possess distinct characteristics that define their unwavering commitment to their vision. First and foremost, they exhibit a remarkable clarity of vision, deeply understanding the principles driving every action and decision. Their passion and sense of purpose are insightful, as they are driven by an intense dedication to advancing their cause, regardless of the obstacles they may encounter.

Resilience and perseverance are trademarks of their character. In the face of setbacks and adversity, they remain steadfast in their commitment and undeterred by challenges. Courage and conviction fuel their resolve, enabling them to stand firm in pursuing their principles, even in the face of opposition or criticism. Additionally, they demonstrate adaptability and flexibility, recognizing that achieving their vision requires innovative thinking and the willingness to embrace change. Empathy and compassion characterize their interactions. They lead by example, inspiring others to join them in their cause through their authenticity, integrity, and inspiring leadership.

A Visionary leader's dedication to lifelong service profoundly impacts the leaders themselves and their families, teams, and people worldwide. At the core of their commitment lies a deep sense of purpose and conviction, driving them to dedicate their lives to a cause greater than themselves. For the leader, this dedication becomes central to their identity, shaping their values, decisions, and actions. It brings fulfillment and satisfaction derived from making a meaningful impact on the world, but it also entails sacrifices—time away from loved ones, emotional strain, and relentless effort. This dedication to lifelong service has profound effects that extend beyond the individual to their family, team, and the broader community worldwide.

Dedication Impacts Others

For the Visionary leader, a lifelong commitment to service often shapes their identity and sense of purpose. It gives them a deep fulfillment and satisfaction derived from positively impacting the world. However, it can also come with personal sacrifices, including time away from family, emotional strain, and physical exhaustion. Despite these challenges, the leader is driven by their unwavering dedication to their vision and the belief that their efforts contribute to the greater good.

But how does the greater good compare to a leader's close loved ones? As it turns out, the dedication of a Visionary leader to lifelong service can have positive and challenging effects on their family. On one hand, the family may feel proud of the leader's accomplishments and inspired by their commitment to making a difference. However, they may also experience periods of separation, stress, and uncertainty as the leader devotes significant time and energy to their work. Family members may need to adapt to a lifestyle that revolves around the leader's mission, which can create opportunities for growth and moments of difficulty.

By contrast, witnessing the dedication to lifelong service within the Visionary leader's team is a powerful engine for inspiration and motivation. It instills a shared sense of purpose and commitment among team members, driving them to work tirelessly toward common goals. These leaders' examples set a high standard for dedication and perseverance, encouraging the team to overcome obstacles with resilience and determination. Also, the leader's commitment to service builds a positive organizational culture built on trust, collaboration, and a collective pursuit of global impact.

Their service has a ripple effect extending beyond their immediate circle. Through their work, they inspire others to take action, effecting positive change in their communities and beyond. Their influence may catalyze movements, spark innovations, and challenge the status quo, ultimately shaping the course of history. Additionally, the leader's dedication to service may inspire future generations of leaders to follow in their footsteps, creating a legacy of impact that endures for years to come.

Visionaries who dedicate their lives to their principles typically possess unique characteristics that drive their unwavering commitment to their vision. These characteristics include.

Clear Vision | Visionaries have a clear and compelling vision of the future they want to create. They deeply understand their principles and values, which guide their decision-making and actions.

Passion and Purpose | Visionaries are deeply passionate about their principles and purpose. A sense of mission drives them to dedicate their lives to advancing their cause, regardless of their challenges.

Resilience and Perseverance | Visionaries demonstrate resilience and perseverance in pursuing their principles. They are undeterred by setbacks or obstacles and remain steadfast in their commitment, even when faced with adversity.

Courage and Conviction | Visionaries exhibit courage and conviction in standing up for their principles despite opposition or criticism. They are willing to take risks and challenge the status quo to bring about positive change.

Adaptability and Flexibility | Visionaries are adaptable and flexible in their approach. They recognize that achieving their principles may require experimentation, innovation, and course corrections.

Empathy and Compassion | Visionaries demonstrate empathy and compassion towards others. They seek to understand the needs and perspectives of those affected by their principles and strive to create solutions that benefit the greater good.

Think Different | Visionaries are innovative thinkers unafraid to think outside the box. They constantly seek new ways to advance their principles and are open to exploring unconventional ideas and approaches.

Inspirational Leadership | Visionaries inspire others to join them in their cause through their leadership and example. They can articulate their vision in a way that resonates with others and mobilizes support for their principles.

Integrity and Authenticity | Visionaries operate with integrity and authenticity, aligning their actions with their principles and values. They are transparent in their motivations and hold themselves to high ethical standards.

Long-Term Vision | Visionaries take a long-term perspective in their efforts to advance their principles. They understand that meaningful change takes time and are committed to staying the course, even when progress may be slow.

Continuous Learning | Visionary leaders are lifelong learners. They seek personal and professional growth opportunities and encourage others to do the same.

These qualities are not inherited but developed through experiences, education, and self-awareness. While some people may naturally possess certain traits, such as empathy or creativity, others can cultivate these qualities through deliberate effort and practice. Leaders who do so have a deep understanding of their purpose and a clear vision of the future they seek to create. They exhibit courage in the face of uncertainty, resilience in adversity, and empathy in their interactions with others, and they embrace a commitment to lifelong growth.

Dedication Is Rare

Despite the transformative impact these qualities can have, relatively few people inherit them. There are several reasons for this scarcity. Firstly, developing these traits often requires intentional effort and self-awareness, which only some possess. Additionally, fear of failure and a preference for comfort and stability can inhibit individuals from taking risks or challenging the status quo. Short-term thinking and focusing on immediate gratification may also overshadow the long-term vision and impact that Visionary leaders prioritize. Also, cultural norms and conditioning can discourage individuals from embracing these qualities and managing these core principles.

In essence, while the principles of Visionary leadership hold immense potential for driving positive change and innovation, their acquisition requires deliberate cultivation and a willingness to depart from conventional norms. By fostering an environment that encourages self-awareness, risk-taking, and authenticity, we can empower more individuals to embody these qualities and lead with vision and purpose.

So why do so few people inherit these lifelong Visionary qualities? Several factors contribute to this:

Lack of Self-Awareness | Many people may not know their strengths, weaknesses, or values, making it difficult for them to develop a clear vision or lead authentically.

Fear of Failure | Fear of failure can prevent people from taking risks or pursuing ambitious goals. Visionary leaders embrace failure as a natural part of the learning process and use it as an opportunity for growth.

Comfort with the Status Quo | Some individuals may be content with the status quo and reluctant to challenge existing norms or push boundaries. Visionary leaders are disruptors who are willing to challenge the status quo and drive change.

Short-term Thinking | Many people focus on short-term gains or immediate gratification rather than long-term goals or lasting impact. Visionary leaders think strategically and prioritize long-term sustainability over short-term rewards.

Although most Visionary leaders possess at least some of these qualities as an instinctive part of their being, anyone willing to put in the effort can develop and cultivate these traits. By embracing courage, resilience, empathy, and innovation, individuals can unlock their potential to become Visionary leaders and positively impact the world.

Why Dedication Matters

Visionary leaders are like architects of the future, orchestrating complex endeavors with the precision of a Swiss watch. What keeps that watch ticking through endless challenges and setbacks is the dedication they carry in their heart—dedication to their values, to their community, and above all to their vision for the future. They possess an unwavering belief in their goals and a keen understanding of the intricate mechanisms required to turn aspirations into reality. They inspire their teams with a shared sense of purpose, empowering them to overcome obstacles and deliver extraordinary results.

By fusing Visionary dedication with the other qualities of Visionary DNA, these leaders create organizations that are unfailingly true to their vision. Their selfless effort and creativity set them apart, enabling them to achieve their audacious goals and shape a future that matches their aspirations.

Visionaries are often misunderstood and underestimated, but they make a real difference in the world. They inspire us to dream big and never give up on our goals.

Inspire. Aspire. Be Great.

The Visionary | MAHATMA GANDHI

You must be the change you wish to see in the world.
– Mahatma Gandhi

Mahatma Gandhi, born Mohandas Karamchand Gandhi on October 2, 1869, in Porbandar, India, was a preeminent leader of the Indian independence movement against British colonial rule. His life was marked by an unwavering dedication to nonviolent resistance, civil disobedience, and the principles of truth and justice.

Gandhi was born into a Hindu merchant caste family and received his law education in London. After returning to India, he struggled with discrimination against Indians in South Africa, where he worked as a lawyer. It was here that Gandhi first developed his philosophy of *satyagraha*, or "truth force," which emphasized the power of nonviolent resistance to injustice.

Upon his return to India in 1915, Gandhi emerged as a leader in the Indian National Congress, advocating for the rights of Indians and challenging British rule. He led numerous nonviolent civil disobedience campaigns, including the famous Salt March in 1930, which protested the British salt monopoly and galvanized support for Indian independence. Gandhi emphasized the importance of self-discipline, simplicity, and service to others throughout his life. He promoted communal harmony and religious tolerance, advocating for the rights of marginalized groups such as Dalits (formerly known as "untouchables") and women.

Gandhi's commitment to nonviolence and his unwavering adherence to truth inspired millions worldwide and earned him the title of "Mahatma," meaning "Great Soul." He led by example, living a life of strictness and humility, and became a symbol of hope and resistance against oppression.

Despite facing numerous arrests, imprisonments, and physical attacks, Gandhi remained dedicated to his principles and pursued his goal of Indian independence through peaceful means. His efforts culminated in India's independence from British rule on August 15, 1947. However, it was accompanied by the partition of India and the creation of Pakistan, leading to collective violence and displacement.

Gandhi faced numerous barriers and consequences throughout his life as he pursued his social and political change mission through nonviolent resistance and civil disobedience. One of the most significant challenges he encountered was opposition from the British colonial authorities, who viewed his activism as threatening their rule. The authorities and their supporters would arrest him multiple times and subject him to harassment, imprisonment, and violence. These actions often resulted in personal hardship for Gandhi and his followers, including physical injuries and loss of freedom.

Gandhi also faced resistance and criticism from various sectors of Indian society, including conservative elements opposed to his progressive views on caste, religion, and gender equality. Some factions within the Indian National Congress were also skeptical of his strategies and goals. Gandhi's commitment to nonviolence and willingness to engage in dialogue with adversaries sometimes led to internal divisions and disagreements within the independence movement.

Additionally, Gandhi's advocacy for interfaith harmony and communal unity was challenged by religious extremists and communal tensions, particularly during the partition of India in 1947. The violence and bloodshed that accompanied partition deeply troubled Gandhi, and he fasted to promote peace and reconciliation between Hindus and Muslims.

Despite these barriers and challenges, Gandhi remained dedicated to his principles and unwavering in his commitment to nonviolence and truth. His resilience in the face of adversity and his ability to maintain moral integrity amidst turmoil inspired millions and earned him the respect and admiration of people worldwide. Gandhi's legacy continues to serve as a beacon of hope and inspiration for those fighting for justice, peace, and equality. Tragically, Gandhi was assassinated by a Hindu nationalist on January 30, 1948, while on his way to evening prayers in New Delhi. His death was mourned worldwide, and he is remembered as one of the greatest leaders and visionaries of the 20th century, whose legacy continues to inspire movements for social justice and human rights globally.

Mahatma Gandhi is widely regarded as a Visionary leader for his pivotal role in India's struggle for independence and his philosophy of nonviolent resistance. Gandhi's admired status stems from many remarkable characteristics that defined his persona and leadership throughout his life:

Commitment to Nonviolence | Gandhi's unwavering commitment to nonviolence, or *ahimsa*, was central to his philosophy and actions. He believed in the power of nonviolent resistance to achieve social and political change, even in the face of oppression and injustice. Gandhi's philosophy of nonviolent resistance, or satyagraha, inspired countless individuals and movements worldwide. His approach to civil disobedience and peaceful protest became a powerful tool for social and political change, influencing leaders such as Martin Luther King Jr. in the United States and Nelson Mandela in South Africa.

Integrity and Truthfulness | Gandhi was known for his honesty, integrity, and moral rectitude. He lived his life following his principles and held himself to the highest ethical standards. His commitment to truthfulness earned him the title of "Mahatma."

Simplicity and Humility | Gandhi embraced a simple, austere lifestyle, avoiding material possessions and extravagance. He lived modestly, wearing traditional Indian clothing and advocating for self-sufficiency and self-reliance.

Empathy and Compassion | Gandhi demonstrated empathy and compassion towards others, particularly the marginalized and oppressed. He advocated for the rights of Dalits, women, and other disadvantaged groups, and worked tirelessly to alleviate their suffering.

Courage and Fearlessness | Gandhi remained steadfast and resolute in his convictions despite facing numerous challenges and threats to his safety. He displayed remarkable courage and fearlessness in pursuing justice and freedom, inspiring others to overcome their fears and obstacles.

Leadership by Example | Gandhi led by example, embodying the principles of humility, self-sacrifice, and service to others. He lived a life of simplicity and service, demonstrating that authentic leadership is rooted in moral integrity and selflessness. Gandhi's personal integrity, humility, and commitment to truth served as a model of moral leadership for generations to come. He led by example, living a simple and austere life, and his unwavering adherence to his principles earned him the respect and admiration of people worldwide.

Spiritual and Moral Vision | Gandhi's leadership was deeply rooted in his spiritual and moral beliefs. He believed in the inherent dignity and worth of every human being and strove to create a society based on principles of equality, justice, and compassion.

Commitment to Service | Gandhi dedicated his life to serving others and working towards improving society. He viewed service as a moral imperative and encouraged others to join him in pursuing social and political change through constructive action.

Strategic Leadership | Gandhi was a strategic leader who carefully planned and executed nonviolent resistance campaigns. His ability to mobilize the masses through movements like the Salt March and civil disobedience campaigns showcased his strategic acumen.

These characteristics made Mahatma Gandhi an admired figure in India and worldwide. His teachings and philosophy inspire people to strive for a more just, peaceful, and compassionate world. Gandhi's Visionary leadership is characterized by his **commitment to moral behavior, simplicity of lifestyle, inclusive leadership, empathy, strategic acumen, leading by example, religious tolerance**, and **unfailing dedication to his principles**. His influence resonates globally as a symbol of nonviolent social and political change, and he remains an enduring symbol of resistance to oppression and an inspiration of hope for those striving for a more just and peaceful world.

ACCOMPLISHMENTS

Nonviolent Resistance (Satyagraha) | Gandhi is best known for his philosophy of nonviolent resistance, which he called "satyagraha." He led numerous successful civil disobedience campaigns, such as the Quit India Movement, which was instrumental in India's struggle for independence from British colonial rule.

Vision | Gandhi's vision for India went beyond political independence; he sought *swaraj*, meaning self-rule or self-governance. His vision included economic and social empowerment, emphasizing the importance of self-sufficiency and community development.

Indian Independence | Gandhi was pivotal in India's struggle for independence from British colonial rule. Through his leadership of the Indian National Congress and his advocacy of nonviolent resistance, he mobilized millions of Indians in the fight against British imperialism. His efforts ultimately led to India's independence in 1947.

Salt March (1930) | Gandhi's 240-mile Salt March to the Arabian Sea is one of his most iconic acts of civil disobedience. The protest aimed to challenge the British monopoly on salt production and sales by producing salt from seawater. The Salt March galvanized the Indian population and drew international attention to the Indian independence movement.

Social Justice | Gandhi was a tireless advocate for social justice, working to eradicate various forms of discrimination, including untouchability, caste-based discrimination, and gender inequality. He promoted the idea of *sarvodaya*, or "the welfare of all," and worked to uplift marginalized and oppressed communities.

Self-Sufficiency | Gandhi advocated for *swadeshi*, or the use of locally produced goods, and the development of village industries. He encouraged economic self-sufficiency to reduce India's economic dependence on the British Empire.

Unity and Communal Harmony | Gandhi worked to foster unity and communal harmony in a diverse and divided country. He worked to eradicate caste discrimination and promoted the upliftment of the oppressed through education and empowerment. He also believed in interfaith dialogue and promoted religious tolerance and coexistence. His commitment to religious pluralism and his respect for diverse religious traditions continue to inspire efforts toward interfaith dialogue and cooperation.

International Advocacy | Gandhi's message of nonviolence and civil disobedience resonated globally. He was a key figure in the international peace movement. He influenced leaders like Martin Luther King Jr. and Nelson Mandela, who adopted nonviolent resistance in their civil rights and justice struggles.

End of British Rule | Gandhi's leadership in the Indian independence movement and his use of nonviolent resistance played a pivotal role in India's gaining independence from British colonial rule in 1947. India's struggle for independence inspired other nations in their quests for self-determination.

Global Human Rights | Gandhi's commitment to nonviolence and advocacy for justice and human rights left a lasting impact on the global struggle for human rights and social justice. His methods of civil disobedience and peaceful protest continue to inspire movements worldwide.

Legacy of Peace and Nonviolence | Gandhi's legacy endures as a symbol of peace, nonviolence, and moral leadership. His birthday, October 2, is observed as the International Day of Non-Violence.

Chapter 17 | The PURPOSE

Where there is no vision, the people perish.
– Proverbs 29:18 (KJV)

Visionary leaders who integrate faith into their leadership approach build their businesses, grow their culture, and inspire passion in their teams by aligning their actions with a higher mission—they serve a greater purpose than profit. Purpose is not necessarily the same as religious faith. Still, the two are undeniably intertwined, and by studying leaders and organizations that are driven earnestly by faith, we can learn a great deal about how purpose makes the difference in Visionary leadership.

Faith-driven purpose serves as a moral compass, guiding business decisions with integrity and fostering a brand identity grounded in core values such as service, empathy, and community. Leaders who follow such purpose cultivate a culture where team members find deeper meaning in their work, contributing to a shared vision that aligns with their values. By modeling servant leadership and focusing on the well-being of their employees and customers, Visionary leaders create an environment of trust, engagement, and loyalty.

This sense of purpose drives long-term business success. It builds a passionate, motivated team that feels connected to a more significant cause, ensuring the company thrives while maintaining integrity.

Purpose Drives Leadership

Visionary leaders harness the power of purpose to create transformative business environments. They understand that a strong sense of purpose acts as a beacon, aligning team efforts towards a shared goal that transcends mere profit. These leaders build a culture where faith—a deep-seated dedication to the company's mission and potential as well as to a higher spiritual or philosophical calling—permeates every aspect of the organization.

By clearly articulating and consistently reinforcing the company's purpose, Visionary leaders inspire their teams to see their work as more than just a job; as a result, teams view their contributions as meaningful contributions to a more significant cause. This sense of purpose encourages a core motivation, driving employees to go above and beyond in their roles. Actionable faith in the company's vision encourages risk-taking and innovation, as team members feel empowered to explore new ideas and push boundaries.

Visionary leaders also use purpose to inform decision-making at all levels, ensuring that every action aligns with the company's core values and long-term objectives. This consistency builds trust and credibility, both internally and externally. These leaders model resilience and determination by demonstrating unwavering faith in facing challenges and inspiring their teams to persevere through difficulties.

Purpose Grows Leadership

A sense of purpose has effects that ripple out far beyond a leader: a strong sense of purpose helps attract and retain top talent who share the company's values. It creates a magnetic culture where passionate individuals can find meaning in their work and connect with like-minded team members. This shared passion becomes a powerful force for growth and innovation, propelling the business forward.

Ultimately, by integrating purpose through faith into the fabric of their organizations, Visionary leaders create **resilient, adaptable,** and **passionate** teams capable of achieving extraordinary results and making a lasting impact in their industries and communities. Visionary leaders who incorporate **purpose-driven leadership** build their brand, team, and themselves by aligning their actions, values, and decisions with a higher calling.

Visionary leaders with a clearly defined purpose instill transformative characteristics into their brand, team members, and themselves, shaping their organizations and the people they lead. Here are the key factors that fuel that transformation:

Purpose-Driven Leadership | Visionary leaders infuse purpose into their brand, often aligning their business with social, environmental, or ethical causes, creating a strong sense of mission within the organization, motivating employees, and creating an emotional connection with customers. Purpose-driven brands are more likely to inspire loyalty and create lasting impact.

Servant Leadership | Visionary leaders prioritize the well-being of their team and customers over personal gain. They practice servant leadership, focusing on serving others and enabling their success. This approach fosters collaboration, loyalty, and community within the organization.

Passionate Vision | Visionary leaders articulate a clear and compelling future state for their brand or company. This vision serves as their guidepost, aligning the team around a shared purpose and motivating everyone toward long-term goals. Leaders inspire others to see beyond the present and work toward a tangible future, inspiring all those aligned with their vision.

Authenticity and Integrity | Leaders with vision are grounded in authenticity, acting consistently with their values and principles. They build trust by being transparent and genuine, strengthening their brand's reputation, and fostering loyalty within their teams. Authenticity in leadership also encourages team members to bring their whole selves to work, promoting a culture of openness and respect.

By embodying these transformative characteristics, Visionary leaders drive their companies toward success and leave a lasting impact on the people they lead, creating a robust and purpose-driven brand and fostering a high-performance culture that thrives on innovation and integrity.

Purpose in Action

The Visionary landscape is abounding with companies that have applied purpose-driven leadership to create incredible success, advancing the status of their brands and their larger faith-based values. Here are just a few of the most prominent examples:

Chick-fil-A, is a company that focuses on service, hospitality, and community, values that are deeply embedded in its brand DNA. The company's purpose-driven approach, rooted in Christian faith, helps build strong customer loyalty and a clear identity. Truett Cathy, the founder of Chick-fil-A, consistently emphasized that his faith guided his business decisions, such as closing stores on Sundays to allow employees time for worship and rest. His faith shaped his leadership style and the long-term success of his brand.

Hobby Lobby, founded on biblical principles, encourages employees to prioritize family and faith, creating a supportive and purpose-driven workplace. This focus on work-life balance and shared values fosters a loyal, motivated workforce. David Green, the company's founder, built a legacy of faith-based entrepreneurship by ensuring his company's success was tied to generosity, supporting ministries, and preserving family values. His purpose-driven approach ensures the company's influence extends far beyond profit.

In-N-Out Burger, promotes a culture of care for employees and customers. The company fosters a family-like atmosphere led by Christian faith, reflecting the core values of that faith in every interaction, thus contributing to its success and brand loyalty.

Tom's Shoes, with a purpose-driven model of giving a pair of shoes for every pair sold, reflects founder Blake Mycoskie's belief in positively impacting the world. His purpose-aligned leadership has resulted in a business that's not only successful but socially impactful.

So how does a leader transform their own faith into a brand-actionable sense of Visionary purpose? Here's how purpose-driven leaders effectively combine the principles epitomized by the above examples to create lasting success:

Grounding the Brand in Core Values | Faith-based Visionary leaders infuse their brands with values derived from their beliefs, such as integrity, compassion, service, and humility. Their faith provides a clear moral compass, which helps them maintain focus on a purpose beyond profit. This alignment of faith with purpose creates an authentic brand identity, attracting customers who resonate with the brand's mission and ethical standards. The brand becomes a reflection of the leader's values, offering a sense of consistency and trust to both consumers and employees.

Inspiring the Team with a Deeper Sense of Meaning | Visionary leaders leverage their faith to inspire and engage their teams by emphasizing a shared higher purpose. They foster an environment where team members work not only for financial goals but also for a mission that aligns with personal values. By modeling servant leadership, these leaders encourage a culture of service, empathy, and mutual respect. Employees feel more connected to their work when it aligns with something meaningful, and leaders who integrate faith create a work environment that emphasizes community, support, and personal growth.

Developing Themselves Through Faith | Faith provides Visionary leaders with personal guidance and strength, helping them build resilience, humility, and empathy. They view leadership as a calling, and their faith is a constant source of inspiration and motivation, especially in times of challenge. This inner grounding helps them make decisions with integrity, maintain modesty, and keep their focus on long-term impact rather than short-term success. By relying on their faith, they are better able to lead with purpose and build a legacy that aligns with their spiritual beliefs.

Creating a Purpose-Driven, Faith-Inspired Culture | Visionary leaders use faith and purpose to shape their organizational culture. They promote values like honesty, kindness, and service, which flow directly from their faith and purpose. This culture often leads to greater employee engagement, reduced turnover, and increased productivity. Team members are inspired to bring their best selves to work, knowing their efforts contribute to something meaningful. Purpose-driven leadership and faith create a positive environment where people feel valued for who they are, not just what they produce.

Making Purpose-Aligned Business Decisions | Faith and purpose-driven leaders prioritize decisions that align with their ethical and spiritual values. They often sacrifice short-term profits for long-term integrity and mission fulfillment. These leaders are guided by fairness, stewardship, and community responsibility, ensuring their business decisions reflect their beliefs. This strengthens the brand's reputation and attracts customers, employees, and partners who share those values.

Leaving a Lasting Legacy | Leaders who incorporate faith and purpose-driven leadership build a legacy long after their time at the company. By focusing on principles that align with their beliefs, they establish a brand and culture that resonate deeply with employees and customers. Their positive impact on the community often shapes their legacy, the lives they improve, and the integrity with which they lead. This long-term approach to leadership creates enduring success as the company continues to thrive on the foundational values set by the leader.

Building Stronger Communities | Faith-based, purpose-driven leaders often extend their influence beyond the business to benefit broader communities. They engage in charitable initiatives, social impact projects, and community support efforts, creating a ripple effect that enhances their brand's reputation and fosters goodwill. By prioritizing service to others, these leaders reinforce the connection between their faith, purpose, and their company's positive role in the world.

Why Purpose Matters

Visionary leaders who integrate faith with purpose-driven leadership can build brands that are not only profitable but also profoundly impactful. By grounding their decisions and actions in a higher calling, they inspire teams, create strong organizational cultures, and ensure that their brand reflects the values they hold dear. This approach leads to business success and contributes to personal growth, team development, and a lasting legacy.

Follow. Believe. Lead.

The Visionary | JESUS

Let us not become weary in doing good, for at the proper time
we will reap a harvest if we do not give up.
– **Galatians 6:9**

The single most Visionary trait of Jesus Christ is his unwavering commitment to a transformative mission of love and redemption. Jesus had a clear and revolutionary vision to reconcile humanity with God, centered on unconditional love, grace, and forgiveness. This vision transcended cultural, religious, and social barriers, radically reshaping how people related to each other and God. His teachings, such as loving one's enemies, forgiving endlessly, and serving others selflessly, were not just philosophical ideals— they were transformative actions aimed at creating a more just, compassionate, and spiritually renewed world. This Visionary trait, embodied in his message and life, has continued inspiring individuals and movements for over 2,000 years.

Born in Bethlehem around 4 B.C., Jesus of Nazareth is the central figure of Christianity, regarded by believers as the Son of God and the promised Messiah. His life and teachings, as recorded in the New Testament, have shaped countless societies' spiritual, moral, and ethical frameworks throughout history. Raised in Nazareth, Jesus began his public ministry around 30, preaching about the Kingdom of God, love, forgiveness, and repentance. He embarked on three years of teaching, preaching, and performing miracles throughout Galilee and Judea. His teachings focused on love, forgiveness, repentance, and the Kingdom of God. He delivered public addresses such as the Sermon on the Mount, including the Beatitudes and other moral and ethical living teachings.

Jesus' revolutionary teachings challenged both religious and social norms, gaining him followers and critics alike. He also performed numerous miracles, including healing the sick, raising the dead, and feeding multitudes, further establishing his divine authority. His ministry culminated in his crucifixion in Jerusalem, a sacrifice Christians believe was made to atone for the sins of humanity.

According to the Gospels, Jesus rose from the dead three days later, affirming his victory over sin and death. His resurrection is celebrated as the cornerstone of the Christian faith. This event, known as the Resurrection, is celebrated by Christians worldwide as the cornerstone of their faith. He ascended into heaven after appearing to his disciples, leaving them with the Great Commission to spread his teachings worldwide.

Jesus' life, death, and resurrection continue to inspire millions, with his message of love, salvation, and hope influencing religious thought and the course of world history. His life and teachings are primarily recorded in the four Gospels—Matthew, Mark, Luke, and John—which recount his ministry, miracles, death, and resurrection.

The life of Jesus Christ continues to be a source of inspiration, hope, and spiritual guidance for billions of people across the globe.

His teachings on love, compassion, forgiveness, and salvation have profoundly influenced individuals, societies, and cultures throughout history, making him one of the most influential figures in human history.

For our purposes, Jesus Christ is regarded as a Visionary leader due to the profound impact of his teachings and the enduring legacy of his leadership. While his leadership style may differ from traditional corporate or political leaders, several aspects of his life and ministry exemplify Visionary leadership:

Clear Vision and Purpose | Jesus articulated a clear vision for his mission on Earth, which centered around love, compassion, and the Kingdom of God. His teachings emphasized forgiveness, humility, and service principles, envisioning a world transformed by faith and righteousness.

Innovative Thinking | Jesus employed innovative methods to communicate his message, often using parables, storytelling, and symbolic actions to convey profound spiritual truths. His approach challenged conventional wisdom and inspired people to think differently about their lives and relationships.

Empowering Others | Jesus empowered his followers to become leaders in their own right, encouraging them to spread his message and embody his teachings through their actions. He invested in their growth and development, mentoring them to fulfill their potential and carry on his mission after his departure.

Courage and Resilience | Jesus demonstrated remarkable courage and resilience in the face of opposition and adversity. Despite facing persecution, rejection, and ultimately, crucifixion, he remained steadfast in his commitment to his vision and purpose, inspiring others to persevere in their struggles.

Servant Leadership | Jesus exemplified the principles of servant leadership, prioritizing the needs of others above his own interests and leading by example through acts of compassion, humility, and self-sacrifice. His life was a testament to the power of love and service to transform lives and communities.

Global Impact | Jesus' leadership transcended cultural and geographical boundaries, influencing countless individuals and societies across time and place. His teachings continue to shape the moral and ethical framework of diverse cultures and religions worldwide, illustrating the enduring impact of his Visionary leadership.

Fostering Inclusivity and Diversity | Jesus welcomed people from all walks of life into his ministry, regardless of their social status, ethnicity, or background. Visionary leaders can similarly promote inclusivity and diversity within their brands by creating a culture of acceptance, respect, and belonging, making their organization a place where everyone feels valued and empowered to contribute.

Forgiveness and Compassion | Jesus taught the importance of forgiveness, compassion, and reconciliation, even in adversity. Visionary leaders can cultivate a culture of forgiveness and compassion within their organizations, fostering empathy, understanding, and collaboration among team members.

Leading by Example | Above all, Jesus led by example, embodying the values and principles he preached in his own life and actions. Visionary leaders can likewise lead by example, demonstrating humility, resilience, and a commitment to service in their leadership style.

Visionary leaders can apply the teachings of Jesus Christ in various aspects of their leadership approach, drawing inspiration from his example of **compassion, humility,** and **service.** By using the teachings of Jesus Christ, Visionary leaders can create organizations that prioritize **empathy, integrity,** and **purpose,** ultimately fostering a positive impact on their teams, communities, and the world at large.

As a Visionary leader, Jesus demonstrated the qualities of someone who saw beyond his present circumstances and worked towards a transformative future. His teachings inspire and guide millions, making him a powerful example of Visionary leadership. Jesus' leadership, life, and teachings have profoundly shaped human history and inspired generations of followers to strive for a better world.

ACCOMPLISHMENTS

Founding a Global Faith | Jesus established the foundations of Christianity, which has grown into one of the world's largest and most influential religions. His teachings, centered on love, faith, and salvation, have inspired billions of followers across centuries and continents, forming a global community that transcends cultural, ethnic, and geographical boundaries.

Transforming Ethical and Moral Values | Jesus introduced a revolutionary ethical framework, including the commandment to "love your neighbor as yourself" and "love your enemies." These teachings challenged conventional thinking on justice, revenge, and relationships, promoting forgiveness, compassion, and humility as guiding principles, which continue to shape modern moral and ethical systems.

Empowering Ordinary People | Jesus chose and empowered ordinary individuals—fishermen, tax collectors, and others—to carry out his mission. This empowerment of everyday people, combined with the message of equality before God, inspired countless generations to live purposeful lives and spread his teachings, regardless of social standing.

The Resurrection and Promise of Eternal Life | Jesus' resurrection is central to Christian belief, representing victory over sin and death. This event reinforced his message of eternal life and redemption, offering hope and transforming the outlook of his followers toward life, death, and the afterlife. It also provided a concrete validation of his vision of salvation for humanity.

Servant Leadership | Jesus' leadership model was Visionary in overturning traditional concepts of power. Instead of ruling with authority, he served others, washing his disciples' feet and emphasizing humility and service as the highest forms of leadership. His example has influenced countless leaders and organizations that seek to emulate his servant-leader approach.

Conclusion | The OPPORTUNITY

A pessimist sees the difficulty in every opportunity; an optimist sees the opportunity in every difficulty.

– Winston Churchill

As we've seen over the last several chapters, Visionary leaders possess exemplary traits that serve as valuable insight for aspiring leaders. However, their clear and compelling vision is underlying every aspect of their DNA. Visionary leaders have a keen sense of purpose and direction, inspiring others to rally around a shared goal. They demonstrate courage in the face of adversity, showing resilience and determination to overcome obstacles. By learning from the traits of these Visionaries, aspiring leaders can develop the skills and qualities necessary to drive meaningful change, inspire others, and lead with impact. Hopefully, after studying some of the great Visionary leaders who have come before, you are now set to begin your own journey to this elite class of individuals.

This should be well established by now, but it bears emphasizing that <u>this journey is anything but easy</u>. Becoming a Visionary leader is a transformative journey fraught with barriers that impede leaders' progress.

One significant challenge—in fact, the problem I see most frequently in my work with aspiring Visionary leaders—is the absence of that clear and compelling vision. Without a concrete idea of what it is they want to accomplish, many leaders struggle to articulate a future direction for their organization or team, hindering their ability to inspire and mobilize others toward a common goal.

Additionally, fear of failure can paralyze leaders, preventing them from taking risks and pursuing bold initiatives necessary for Visionary leadership. Resistance to change within the organization or team can also pose a formidable barrier, as entrenched attitudes and processes may stifle innovation and progress.

Short-term thinking is another obstacle, with leaders prioritizing immediate results over long-term strategic goals, inhibiting visionary thinking and planning. Moreover, lacking empathy and effective communication can hinder leaders from connecting with their team members and fostering a shared sense of purpose and commitment. Some leaders struggle with relinquishing control and empowering their team members, leading to micromanagement and stifling creativity. Overcoming these barriers demands soul-searching, courage, and a commitment to personal growth, enabling leaders to unlock their visionary potential and drive transformative change within their organizations.

But mark my words: conventional leaders can transform into Visionary leaders by embracing their principles and cultivating practices that promote innovation, foresight, and purpose-driven action. Broadly speaking, there are five main steps that one must follow to achieve Visionary status:

First, cultivating a clear vision is essential. These leaders must envision a compelling future that inspires and motivates them and others. This vision should be ambitious yet attainable, influencing their actions and decisions.

Second, leaders must adopt a mindset of continuous learning and growth. They should seek new knowledge, perspectives, and experiences that broaden their horizons and deepen their understanding of their business, cultures, and the world. They can uncover innovative solutions to complex challenges and adapt to changing circumstances by staying curious and open-minded.

Third, leaders need to prioritize integrity and authenticity in all their interactions. They should lead by example, demonstrating honesty, transparency, and ethical behavior in their personal and professional lives. Building trust and credibility with others is crucial for rallying support around their vision and fostering collaboration and teamwork.

Fourth, these leaders should also cultivate resilience and perseverance in the face of adversity. They should embrace failure as a natural part of the learning process and view setbacks as opportunities for growth and development. By maintaining a positive attitude and resilience in the face of challenges, they can overcome obstacles and stay focused on their long-term goals.

Finally, conventional leaders should foster a culture of innovation and creativity within their teams and organizations. They should encourage experimentation, risk-taking, and out-of-the-box thinking, empowering others to challenge the status quo and pursue bold ideas. By fostering an environment that values innovation and encourages diverse perspectives, they can unlock the full potential of their team and drive meaningful change.

Becoming Visionary

So, how exactly does one accomplish those five steps and develop the 16 Visionary DNA aspects we've studied? If it were something you could pick up in a book, surely Visionaries would be much thicker on the ground! There's no substitute for experience, that great teacher. The first step on your journey to Visionary status is to try, knowing you will likely fail. Whatever happens, you'll be rewarded with a learning opportunity.

While this book can't turn you into a Visionary overnight, it can use some of history's greatest examples of leadership to provide a road map for your Visionary journey. Conventional leaders have the potential to become Visionary by adopting specific strategies and cultivating key qualities in their lives, thinking, actions, and principles:

Clarify your Vision | Visionary leaders have a clear sense of purpose and direction. Ordinary leaders can develop their vision by reflecting on their values, passions, and long-term goals. Articulate a compelling vision that inspires and motivates both yourself and others.

Think Long-Term | Visionary leaders think beyond immediate challenges and opportunities. Ordinary leaders can adopt a long-term perspective by considering the broader implications of their decisions and actions. Anticipate future trends, identify emerging opportunities, and envision innovative solutions to address them.

Take Bold Action | Visionary leaders are unafraid to take risks and pursue bold initiatives. Ordinary leaders can demonstrate visionary behavior by stepping out of their comfort zone, embracing uncertainty, and seizing opportunities for growth and innovation. Challenge the status quo and pursue ambitious goals that align with your vision.

Lead with Purpose | Visionary leaders lead with a sense of purpose and authenticity. Ordinary leaders can become visionary by aligning their actions with values and principles. Demonstrate integrity, empathy, and humility in your interactions with others, inspiring trust and building meaningful connections.

Embrace Creativity and Innovation | Visionary leaders foster a culture of creativity and innovation within their organizations. Ordinary leaders can encourage innovation by creating an environment where diverse perspectives are valued, ideas are welcomed, and experimentation is encouraged. Empower your team members to think creatively and explore new possibilities.

Learn Continuously | Visionary leaders are lifelong learners who seek out new knowledge and experiences. Ordinary leaders can cultivate a growth mindset by actively seeking feedback, embracing failure as an opportunity for learning, and investing in their personal and professional development. Be curious, open-minded, and willing to adapt to change.

Inspire Others | Visionary leaders inspire and empower others to contribute to realizing their vision. Ordinary leaders can inspire by communicating their vision effectively, providing mentorship and support to their team members, and recognizing and celebrating their contributions. Create a sense of shared purpose and rally others around common goals.

By adopting these strategies and cultivating these qualities, ordinary leaders can transform into Visionary leaders who inspire others, drive positive change, and leave a lasting impact on their organizations and communities.

Becoming a Visionary leader is a lofty aspiration that often encounters significant barriers. One of the primary challenges is the struggle to develop and communicate a compelling vision. Many leaders struggle to articulate a clear picture of the future, hindering their ability to inspire and rally others toward a common purpose.

Additionally, a failure mindset can be a significant restraint, causing leaders to hesitate to take risks and pursue innovative ideas. Resistance to change within the organization or team can also pose a substantial obstacle, as entrenched attitudes and processes may impede progress and innovation. Moreover, leaders may face challenges in balancing short-term demands with long-term strategic goals, making it challenging to prioritize visionary thinking amid day-to-day pressures. Inefficient communication and empathy are also critical barriers, as leaders must connect with their teams deeply to build trust and alignment around the vision, and must empower them to take risks and bold action on their behalf.

Overcoming these barriers requires courage, resilience, and a willingness to challenge the status quo, but those who successfully navigate these obstacles can unlock their potential as Visionary leaders capable of driving meaningful change and transformation. Visionary leadership requires self-examination and a willingness to learn and grow personally and professionally.

To provide some context and inspiration for your journey to becoming that which you desire, think back to the anecdote that opened this book. Before he was hailed as the savior of Apple and the architect of the modern digital lifestyle, Steve Jobs was brought back to his former company, now in shambles. The perspective and boldness with which he met that challenge changed history.

Jobs said the following in a 1994 interview with the Santa Clara Valley Historical Association:

"When you grow up you tend to get told the world is the way it is and your job is just to live your life inside the world. Try not to bash into the walls too much. Try to have a nice family life, have fun, save a little money.

That's a very limited life. Life can be much broader once you discover one simple fact, and that is: everything around you that you call life was made up by people that were no smarter than you. And you can change it, you can influence it, you can build your own things that other people can use.

The minute that you understand that you can poke life and actually something will, you know if you push in, something will pop out the other side, that you can change it, you can mold it. That's maybe the most important thing. It's to shake off this erroneous notion that life is there and you're just gonna live in it, versus embrace it, change it, improve it, make your mark upon it.

I think that's very important and however you learn that, once you learn it, you'll want to change life and make it better, cause it's kind of messed up, in a lot of ways. Once you learn that, you'll never be the same again."

Enjoy your journey to becoming the person you aspire to be, Visionary! May you inspire others to travel the path you created.

INDEX

INDEX

INDEX

INDEX

ABOUT THE AUTHOR

Bryan Smeltzer is an innovative business leader, bestselling author, and host of *The Visionary Chronicles* podcast. His acclaimed book, *The Visionary Brand*, solidifies his reputation as a transformative leader in brand strategy.

Bryan's diverse career journey spans from aerospace to achieving entrepreneurial success in consumer products, founding and exiting an apparel company before advancing to executive roles with iconic brands such as Oakley, K-Swiss, TaylorMade, and Adidas.

Leveraging his experience in business development, product innovation, and marketing strategy, Bryan now leads LiquidMind, Inc., a cutting-edge brand strategy firm based in Southern California. Here, he empowers innovative brands to disrupt and dominate global markets while eliminating the status quo.

For more information or to connect with Bryan, visit:
BryanSmeltzer.com
LiquidMindsite.com
TheVisionaryFiles.com